The Frank W. Pierce Memorial
Lectureship and Conference Series
Number 7

New Perspectives in Workers' Compensation

Edited by John F. Burton, Jr.

ILR Press
New York State School of
Industrial and Labor Relations
Cornell University

Cover design by Kat Dalton

Library of Congress Cataloging-in-Publication Data

New perspectives in workers' compensation / edited by John F. Burton, Jr.
    p. cm. — (The Frank W. Pierce Memorial lectureship and conference series ; no. 7)
    Bibliography: p.
    Includes index.
    Contents: A tribute to Arthur Larson / John Lewis – Tensions of the next decade / Arthur Larson — Paying for asbestos-related diseases under workers' compensation / Donald N. Dewees — Workers' compensation, wages, and the risk of injury / Ronald G. Ehrenberg — Lessons for the administration of workers' compensation from the social security disability insurance program / Jerry L. Mashaw — The future of workers' compensation / Robert J. Lampman and Robert M. Hutchens.
    ISBN 0-87546-143-3 (alk. paper). — ISBN 0-87546-144-1 (pbk. : alk. paper)
    1. Workers' compensation—United States. I. Burton, John F. II. Series.
HD7103.65.U6N42 1988
368.4′1—dc19

88-37928
CIP

Copies may be ordered from
ILR Press
New York State School of
Industrial and Labor Relations
Cornell University
Ithaca, NY 14851–0952

The paper used in this publication meets the minimum requirements
of American National Standard for Information Sciences—Permanence of
Paper for Printed Library Materials, ANSI Z39.48—1984.   ∞

Printed in the United States of America
5 4 3 2 1

CONTENTS

TABLES AND FIGURES

ACKNOWLEDGMENTS

Most of the chapters in this volume are considerably revised versions of papers presented at a conference held in 1984 at the New York State School of Industrial and Labor Relations at Cornell University (the ILR School). The conference was one of a series held at four sponsoring institutions: Cornell University; Rutgers, the State University of New Jersey; the University of Connecticut; and Syracuse University.

Support for the 1984 conference and publication of this volume was provided in part by the Frank W. Pierce Memorial Lectureship Fund. This fund was established in 1965 to honor Frank W. Pierce, a pioneer in industrial relations, who graduated from Cornell in 1916. Pierce served as head of industrial relations for Standard Oil Company (New Jersey) and was a member of the Advisory Council of the ILR School. The Pierce Fund supports lectures at the ILR School by distinguished scholars and professionals in the field of industrial and labor relations.

The publication of this volume was also supported in part by the Mary Donlon Fund. Mary Donlon was a graduate of the Cornell University Law School and served as chairperson of the agency that administered the New York State workers' compensation program. In 1947–48, she also served as the president of the International Association of Industrial Accident Boards and Commissions (IAIABC), the professional association for workers' compensation administrators. In 1948, the Mary Donlon Fund was established at the ILR School to promote education in the field of workers' compensation and related benefit programs. The first lecture supported by the fund was given by Arthur Larson, a former faculty member of the Cornell Law School and a contributor to this volume.

The list of people with connections to both Cornell University and workers' compensation additionally includes Frances Perkins, who also served as president of the IAIABC in 1928–29 while she was chairperson of the New York State Industrial Board during Governor Franklin D. Roosevelt's administration. President Roosevelt subsequently appointed her secretary of labor, making her the first woman cabinet member. From 1957 until 1965, she was associated with the ILR School as a visiting lecturer.

The 1984 conference and the publication of this volume by the ILR Press thus continue a tradition of interest in workers' compensation by the New York State School of Industrial and Labor Relations and Cornell University.

A TRIBUTE TO ARTHUR LARSON

Arthur Larson has been the dominant legal scholar in the field of workers' compensation for more than a quarter-century. He has also had a distinguished career as a lawyer, a professor, and a government official.

The conference on workers' compensation from which this volume is derived included a dinner honoring Arthur Larson. Excerpts from the speech presented by John Lewis at that event provide an appropriate beginning for this volume, which is dedicated to Arthur Larson with the admiration and affection of his many friends.

I first heard about Arthur Larson when I started as a student at Duke University Law School in 1964, shortly before the Barry Goldwater–Lyndon Johnson election. At that time, Duke was a relatively conservative institution, and when I arrived, many people were upset because Dr. Larson, who was at Duke, supported the Democratic candidate, although he was a leading figure in the Republican party.

Dr. Larson had been undersecretary of labor in the Eisenhower administration and had then moved on to the United States Information Agency and eventually to a position as special assistant to the president. He wrote quite a few of the president's speeches, including his 1956 acceptance speech, and several delivered on the campaign trail.

I met Dr. Larson for the first time while working at Duke's Rule of Law Research Center. The center had grown out of the idea for Law Day during the early 1950s. Charles Rhyne, a Duke graduate and the president of the American Bar Association at the time, con-

ceived of the idea for Law Day and proposed it to President Eisenhower, who liked it. Arthur Larson was given the job of writing the speech and proclamation to announce Law Day, and, as Arthur Larson puts it, "he got hooked."

Mr. Rhyne decided that the concept should be taken a step further and proposed what became the Rule of Law Research Center. He also proposed that Arthur Larson become its director. The discussions over whether Dr. Larson should go to Durham involved many people, including President Eisenhower, who had to give permission for Dr. Larson to leave.

I worked for the Rule of Law Research Center for about a year without knowing very much about Dr. Larson. Then, in the spring of 1965, I was informed that I was under consideration for a job working directly for him. I was called into his office, and we talked for a while. He finally said that he wanted me to work with him on a book on workers' compensation. I, of course, said, "Great," but what went through my mind was, "How big a deal can that be, analyzing some case law about people who got fired and wanted compensation?"

Four months and twelve hundred cases later, I understood what workers' compensation was all about. I also learned the significance of Arthur Larson. In case after case, the only citation of authority was to Arthur Larson, and the only rules of law that were picked up and directly put into the case law were those in Arthur Larson's treatise.

I decided it was time to learn a little more, not only about workers' compensation but about Arthur Larson. I found out, for example, how Arthur Larson became involved with workers' compensation. I learned that he had practiced law for three or four years in Wisconsin and that the partner who handled workers' compensation for the firm had died. As a result, the job was given to the junior associate, who happened to be Arthur Larson. It would be nice to say, "And that connection to workers' compensation continued until this day." In fact, he severed his ties with the field for many years.

The tie was renewed in the 1940s, when Arthur Larson was on the faculty of Cornell University Law School. During that time, Dr. Larson had a bad back, for which he was treated at the Cornell Medical Center in New York. There, he was put in a full-body cast, placed on a train to Ithaca, and told he would be laid up for five or six months. As he described it to me, he had some time on his hands and decided to write a book. He had already written one, a casebook on corporations, and was looking around for a new field. As a last resort, he outlined a book on workers' compensation law.

A treatise is not written overnight; indeed, it took five years of "monastic living" to get it done. It would have been completed a few years earlier, but the publisher, on being presented with a manuscript for one volume, said, "Wait a minute. A treatise is not one volume. Go back to the drawing board, and make that one volume at least two," which Arthur Larson did.

Eventually, the treatise was published, and, as Dr. Larson describes it, "All hell broke loose." The treatise was not only very good, it was the best. A few years after it was published, Dr. Larson was awarded the Henderson Memorial Prize, which is given by Harvard University for the best treatise in the field of administrative law. The same week, he was awarded the Doctorate of Civil Laws from Oxford University, its highest degree.

Dr. Larson has said he is more proud of the treatise than of anything else he has accomplished and that everything else has occurred because of it. He was, for instance, brought into the Eisenhower administration as a result of it, and his public life went on from there.

If I can assign one important attribute to Arthur Larson's treatise, it is not that it is always right, because I do not think it is, but that it provides the perfect framework for analyzing and understanding workers' compensation. There is always the proper niche in which to put a case, always a section that provides the assistance a treatise is supposed to provide. The jobs of the courts and of the legislatures—of everyone who has anything to do with workers' compensation—have been made infinitely easier because he created a treatise with an intellectual structure that organizes the field. To me, that is the most important contribution that anyone can make in any field of law.

1 ·INTRODUCTION

John F. Burton, Jr.

Several new perspectives on workers' compensation are presented in the five subsequent papers in this volume. I shall first briefly summarize these perspectives, then examine them more intensively and place them in a general context of workers' compensation developments.

Arthur Larson argues that the workers' compensation reform movement of the last fifteen years, which dealt largely with inadequate benefits and insufficient coverage, was remarkably successful and, as a result, reform proposals for the next decade must be undertaken from the perspective of a program with generous benefits. From this view, reforms such as integration of workers' compensation benefits with those from other private and public programs deserve serious attention.

One issue that has emerged in the last decade and eluded successful resolution is the compensation of occupational diseases, especially those resulting from exposure to asbestos. Donald Dewees reviews the Canadian experience with the asbestos calamity. The Canadian debate over the role of experience rating in the prevention of occupational diseases provides a new perspective on this issue.

Ronald Ehrenberg examines workers' compensation from an economist's perspective. Although economists have a long tradition of studying workers' compensation, in the last decade there has been a significant increase in the quantity and sophistication of that research. Some of the verities of workers' compensation, such as the beneficial role of experience rating in reducing work-related injuries, appear to some economists to be mere verisimilitudes. Ehrenberg summarizes much of this recent research in a manner accessible to noneconomists and provides a number of useful qualifications.

Workers' compensation is only one of many programs in the workers' disability income system that provide cash benefits, medical care, and rehabilitation services to disabled persons of working age. Workers' compensation can usefully be examined from the perspective of other individual programs in the system or of the entire system.

Jerry Mashaw draws on his knowledge of the disability insurance component of the Social Security program to suggest some lessons for the administration of workers' compensation. From this perspective, Mashaw challenges some of the shibboleths of workers' compensation, such as the undesirability of compromise and release agreements.

Robert Lampman and Robert Hutchens examine the performance of workers' compensation within the workers' disability income system. Although workers' compensation is only a small portion of the system, since 1970 it has maintained its share of cash benefits for disability. Whether this vitality can be maintained is not evident, however, because part of this record was due to the states' efforts in the 1970s to upgrade the program so as to forestall federal intervention, which is no longer a threat. Despite the apparent recent slowdown in the growth of workers' compensation payments and the extensive criticism of the program by researchers and others, Lampman and Hutchens expect that workers' compensation will survive as an independent program because of its broad political support.

Workers' compensation can also be viewed from the perspective of general developments in the economy and society that have implications for its future. Although none of the papers in this volume specifically deals with this perspective, the penultimate section of this chapter provides some relevant information.

The several new perspectives on workers' compensation just introduced suggest the conclusion of this chapter. Those concerned with the future of workers' compensation need a broad perspective that recognizes the relevance of contributions from other programs and various viewpoints and that also recognizes the program's future is intertwined with developments elsewhere in the workers' disability income system and in society.

New Issues in Workers' Compensation

The issues in workers' compensation are evolving. According to Larson, those that dominated in the 1970s have given way to a set of new issues that will provide the primary tensions of the next decade. Larson identifies four such tensions, including the dispute about whether workers' compensation benefits will be the sole remedy of an injured worker against the employer. The shift in major issues has been so complete, according to Larson, that it is now a problem that some "well-intentioned champions of workers' compensation" have not recognized that inadequate benefits and incomplete coverage are no longer general failings of the program.

The Reform Record

Larson's view that the old problems involving benefits and coverage are now generally solved seems overly optimistic. I demur with some hesitation, for clearly most states have significantly improved their laws in the past fifteen years.[1] Still, there are some disturbing aspects of the reform record in these years that warrant examination, since a proper assessment of the agenda for the next decade depends on a correct understanding of where we now are.

States have improved their record of compliance with the nineteen essential recommendations of the National Commission on State Workmen's Compensation Laws. An average compliance score of 6.9 in 1972 has risen to a score of 12.2 in 1988.[2] But almost all that progress was achieved in the first few years after the commission's 1972 report: from 1978 to 1988, the average score increased from 11.6 to only 12.2. And as of 1988, nine states still had not exceeded a compliance score of 9.5—meaning they were not complying with half the national commission's essential recommendations. In 1972,

---

1. Nor do I wish lightly to assume the role of a "well-intentioned champion of workers' compensation," which appears to be a pejorative term in Larson's lexicon.
2. The data in these paragraphs are from U.S. Department of Labor (1988a), as supplemented by U.S. Department of Labor (1988b).

only one state complied with the national commission's recommendation that the maximum weekly benefit for temporary total disability be 100 percent of the state's average weekly wage. By 1980, there were thirty complying states; by 1982, thirty-two states; and then, by 1988, the number slipped back to twenty-nine. Moreover, there are still twelve states where the maximums are less than 75 percent of the state's average weekly wage. There is also a mixed record of compliance with the national commission's recommendation that there be no arbitrary limits of duration or amount for total disability benefits. Only seventeen jurisdictions complied with this recommendation in 1972. By 1978, there were thirty-one complying jurisdictions, but only four more jurisdictions were in compliance by 1988.

These data indicate to me that the quest for adequate workers' compensation benefits is far from over. Moreover, the significant improvement in workers' compensation benefits after 1972 was accompanied by substantial increases in the employers' costs of workers' compensation, from 0.779 percent of payroll in 1972 to 1.290 percent in 1984 (Burton, Hunt, and Krueger 1985). These cost increases make further improvements in state laws more difficult and have generated pressures in several jurisdictions to reduce costs, often by cutting back benefits. Although to date most of these efforts to reduce benefits have been unsuccessful, they suggest a different agenda for the next decade from that envisioned by Larson. In a number of states, there will be a continuing struggle to achieve or maintain adequate benefits, with the likely outcome that, in a significant minority, benefits will remain below the adequacy standards prescribed by the national commission.

Tension over Permanent Partial Benefits

While my assessment of the recent workers' compensation reform effort suggests that one tension of the next decade will be a continuing struggle for adequate benefits, I also believe that the other tensions identified by Larson will be significant. The quest for a better way to compensate workers who suffer from permanent consequences of their injuries, for example, will continue. Much of this debate centers on the proper operational basis for permanent partial disability benefits: shall benefits be based on the extent of the worker's physical impairment (a medical concept) or tied to the extent of the worker's actual loss of wages (an economic concept)? Larson supports the wage-loss approach as the primary basis for benefits, along with a modest cash supplement that compensates the worker for losses in private life.

The wage-loss approach to permanent partial benefits has received much attention in the last decade, in part because of its introduction in Florida and several Canadian jurisdictions. Larson argues that pressures to adopt the wage-loss approach will continue to mount in the coming decade. I agree with this conclusion, although not for the same set of reasons. Larson argues that the wage-loss approach offers the only solution that can demonstrably cut costs. New York's experience with the wage-loss approach for nonscheduled permanent partial disability benefits, however, is that these benefits are quite expensive (see Berkowitz and Burton 1987, 254–57). This suggests that Florida's apparent cost reductions in the wake of the introduction of wage-loss benefits in 1979 are not inherent in the wage-loss approach. I believe the primary justification for the wage-loss approach is not cost savings but the better chance the approach offers of matching benefits to the wage losses caused by work injuries—in Larson's words, "doing a better job of providing the protection which is the system's real reason for existence." Whether improved equity for benefits (rather than reduced costs) is enough to motivate states to adopt the wage-loss approach remains to be seen. One problem with the wage-loss approach that has surfaced in Florida is the difficulty of determining in individual cases whether shortfalls in postinjury earnings are due to the work injury or to other factors. Florida has not completely resolved this problem, and Larson provides suggested statutory language that warrants consideration by any jurisdiction contemplating the wage-loss approach.

The Compensation-Tort Tension

Larson also identifies the tension between workers' compensation and the tort system as one that will be significant in the next decade. Larson discusses the ability of an employee to sue his or her own employer in a tort suit, a recovery action that conflicts with the general principle that workers' compensation is the exclusive remedy of a worker against the employer. Larson surveys six main lines of attack on exclusiveness, including the effort in a few states to stretch the "intentional" injury exception, and concludes that "the doctrine of exclusiveness is in better health today than it was a few years ago."

Despite this recent salutary achievement (at least from the standpoint of employers), the efforts to breach the exclusiveness principle will undoubtedly continue in the next decade, in part because of the general expansion of the tort remedy. Indeed, the tension between workers' compensation and tort law likely to be most significant in the next decade is not the employee's right to sue the employer, but the employee's right to sue other parties as a result of injuries that occur at the workplace. Johns-Manville, for example, filed for bankruptcy protection in large part because of suits from employees of other firms, who are not limited by the exclusiveness principle. The next decade will see a continuing effort to reform the tort laws to limit such suits and perhaps to substitute a general no-fault program that will provide cash benefits and medical care to all who are disabled by exposures to toxic chemicals or other harmful substances. If such reform succeeds, the benefit structure of workers' compensation may have to be drastically revised, at the very least, to mesh with the more general program.

The Federal-State Tension

Larson documents the disappearance of proposed federal standards for the state workers' compensation programs as a conspicuous change from the 1970s to the 1980s. In place of these federal efforts to have a general impact on state workers' compensation laws, the federal-state tension for the next decade is likely to involve attempts for selective federal involvement to deal with occupational diseases. One reason is that tort suits arising from occupational diseases have generated concern among many employers, and labor representatives recognize that the general tort reform movement may provide an opportunity to win concessions in the treatment of workers disabled by occupational diseases in exchange for labor's support of other elements of the reform package. Another reason is that occupational diseases are an emotional topic, and public opinion and politicians are more likely to support reform, even in an era when the national political environment is not particularly conducive to protective legislation. A good example of legislation with prospects enhanced because of the emotional reaction to occupational diseases is the High

Risk Occupational Disease Notification and Prevention Act, which was being considered by Congress as this volume was completed. The basic thrust of the bill is that it would require employers to notify current and former employees about diseases that occur at a disproportionate rate among the employee population of which the employees are members. The idea is to ensure early detection, monitoring, and treatment of occupational diseases. Larson discusses one concern among employers: that the legislation would stimulate a flood of workers' compensation and tort claims.

Regardless of the fate of the High Risk Notification Act, federal legislation to deal with occupational diseases is likely to be a prominent concern in the next decade. Another reason is the tragedy that will play for the balance of the century and continue to draw rage reviews: the thousands of workers who have already been exposed to fatal doses of asbestos and who will develop diseases after latency periods that run for decades. Asbestos has already led to one wave of proposed federal legislation (as discussed by Larson); the enormity of the problem makes it likely that the next decade will include federal efforts to deal with it.

A Canadian Perspective

If federal legislation to compensate workers disabled by asbestos-related diseases is again introduced in the United States, the Canadian experience reviewed by Donald Dewees will provide valuable guidance.

In the United States, the initial decisions about whether to compensate workers are made by employers or insurance carriers, rather than state workers' compensation agencies. The state agencies will resolve disputes between the parties and, in some jurisdictions, will review the payment decisions made by the carriers or employers as cases progress or are closed. Nonetheless, most decisions involving claims handling are made outside the workers' compensation agencies.

In Ontario, claims handling is largely the responsibility of the workers' compensation agency. There are no private carriers or self-insuring (or self-administering) employers as in the United States. One consequence is that the delays and extensive litigation over the issue of liability that are typical in occupational disease cases in United States jurisdictions are likely to be much less common.

The financing mechanisms in the two countries also differ to some degree. In both Ontario and the United States, the workers' compensation program is financed largely by assessments (or premiums) that are paid by employers and that vary by the size of the payroll and by the employer's industry. Use of experience rating at the firm level to further adjust premiums varies between the countries. In most states, firms above a certain size (as measured by premiums) must be experience rated. In Ontario, experience rating of individual firms normally is used only when a majority of firms in the classification vote to use it. There are also limits on the size of the experience-rating surcharge (or credit) for each firm, although the workers' compensation agency can under unusual circumstances impose a higher surcharge.

Dewees provides a useful case study of the use of the Canadian version of experience rating for a Johns-Manville plant in Scarborough, Ontario. The experience rating resulted in premiums that were far less than the benefits paid to workers disabled by asbestos-related diseases contracted at the plant. More provocative is Dewees's conclusion that—given the long latency period for asbestos-related diseases, the impact of corporate taxes on a firm's profits, and the corporate discount rate used to convert future costs and benefits into their present values—even a 100 percent experience rating would have provided little incentive to the Johns-Manville management to avoid exposing workers to asbestos.

This finding is provocative for several reasons. It brings into question one rationale for workers' compensation as a separate program, namely, that experience rating provides incentives for safe workplaces that a general program compensating disabled workers regardless of the source of the disability would not. A related question—assuming that workers' compensation is maintained as a separate program—is whether there is justification for the use of experience rating. Dewees provides several arguments why experience rating may be warranted even if there is no deterrent effect for diseases, but not everyone will find the arguments persuasive. What does seem persuasive is Dewees's conclusion that protection of workers from exposure to hazardous substances requires more than the economic incentives provided by the workers' compensation mechanism;

regulation of these substances by a government agency (such as the Occupational Safety and Health Administration [OSHA] in the United States) is a necessary supplement.

Economists' Perspective

Despite the long history of the involvement of economists in workers' compensation,[3] economic research dealing with the program has been relatively sparse compared to the extensive economic literature dealing with other social insurance programs, such as the unemployment insurance and Social Security programs. One reason for this paucity of economic literature on workers' compensation is the lack of data on the program, especially the lack of comparable data for different states. The unemployment insurance programs in different states have been easier to examine because of the more comparable data the federal presence in that program have produced.

Despite the obstacles to research, economic analyses of the workers' compensation program have significantly increased in the last decade.[4] These economic analyses provide a perspective on workers' compensation that is new to most of the practitioners and scholars in the field, who have a legal background. Ronald Ehrenberg's survey of these studies is valuable because it makes the economist's perspective accessible to noneconomists. For economists, the survey is also useful, because Ehrenberg draws on his own research, which has primarily involved the unemployment insurance program, to point out some of the strengths and weaknesses of the recent economic analyses of workers' compensation.

One issue that economists have examined is the relationship between workers' compensation and workplace safety and health. One of the five basic objectives of workers' compensation pronounced by the National Commission on State Workmen's Compensation Laws is the encouragement of safety. The commission indicated (1972, 15)

---

3. John R. Commons, for example, was both a professor of economics at the University of Wisconsin and a member of the first industrial commission in the state.

4. One explanation for the recent increase in economic research is the increasing utilization of data from private insurance carriers. Private carriers operate in forty-five jurisdictions (including the District of Columbia) and produce a generally comparable data base for use in the rate-making process. Most of these states rely on the National Council on Compensation Insurance (NCCI) for assistance in rate making, and the NCCI data have been used in a number of studies.

that "economic incentives in the program should reduce the number of work-related injuries and diseases."

Ehrenberg indicates that economic theory provides no unambiguous predictions as to whether workers' compensation provides such salutary incentives. Indeed, in the "purest" version of economic theory, in which wages include risk premiums that fully compensate workers for the dangers they face, the introduction of a workers' compensation program or an increase in benefits will merely result in lower wages with no net impact on the behavior of workers or employers.

Once more realistic assumptions are made about the operations of the labor market, such as that workers may have insufficient information about workplace hazards, then conflicting predictions result about the relationship between workers' compensation and safety. If wages do not fully compensate workers for the risks they face, then workers' compensation benefits may increase the cost of labor in risky occupations (since experience rating may increase workers' compensation insurance premiums as a result of the benefits paid to injured workers, while wages may not fall as a result of the higher benefits). The higher costs may in turn lead employers to improve safety in order to bring down their insurance costs. Workers' compensation benefits may also affect worker behavior, however. Workers may take more risks at the workplace if the economic consequences of work injuries are ameliorated by the higher benefits.

The theory just presented is extremely simplified but should convey an essential conclusion from economics, that the theoretical impact of the workers' compensation program on safety is ambiguous. For economists, the ambiguity can be resolved only by empirical investigations, and Ehrenberg also reviews this empirical evidence. There is, for example, evidence that the market produces higher wages in high-risk than in low-risk jobs. Ehrenberg adds a significant qualification, however: that the studies cannot tell whether workers are fully compensated for their risks. In other words, higher-risk jobs may pay more, but the risk premium may be less (or more) than workers would require if they were fully informed about the hazards of various jobs.

If labor markets do not produce fully compensating wage differentials, then the workers' compensation program may have an effect on safety. As indicated above, the theory suggests that higher benefits should have opposite effects on workers and employers. The empirical studies almost invariably show that higher benefits are associated with higher injury rates, indicating that workers' responses dominate over those of employers. One interpretation of this evidence (the "true injury effect") is that higher benefits induce workers to take more risks and thus suffer more injuries. This interpretation suggests that adequate benefits will undermine the safety objective of workers' compensation. Ehrenberg provides an alternative explanation (the "reporting effect") for the positive relationship between benefits and injury rates: that higher benefits do not cause more injuries, just more reporting of those injuries that already occur. This second interpretation does not suggest that adequate benefits undermine the safety objective. As Ehrenberg indicates, the empirical studies have not been able to show which of these explanations of why higher benefits cause more workers' compensation claims is the more accurate.

The data do rather clearly indicate that employee responses to higher benefits dominate over employer responses. This raises questions about the efficacy of experience rating in reducing work injuries. Supplementing the evidence Dewees offered to show the apparent ineffectiveness of experience rating as a promoter of workplace health, most (but not all) studies of the impact of experience rating on safety find no measurable effect.

In addition to providing a useful introduction to economic theory concerning workers' compensation and a critical compendium of the recent empirical studies, Ehrenberg also considers the policy implications of the economic findings. For example, if the positive relationship between higher benefits and higher workers' compensation claims is due at least in part to a true injury effect and not just a reporting effect, then several responses are possible. One is to restructure the program so as to promote safety. The use of more perfect experience rating might increase the economic incentives for employers to reduce workplace hazards, thus offsetting the apparent impact of higher benefits on worker behavior. Another response is to recognize that higher benefits will cause more injuries and to take that consequence into account when deciding the appropriate level of benefits. Recognition that increasingly adequate benefits may lead to increasingly high injury rates does not mean that adequate benefits are an inappropriate goal, only that program designers should recognize that there is a tradeoff between adequacy and injuries and make a conscious value judgment about how the conflict should be resolved.

Workers' Compensation from the Perspective of the Workers' Disability Income System

The workers' disability income system is the set of programs that provide cash benefits, medical care, and rehabilitation services to disabled persons of working age. The workers' compensation program can profitably be examined from the perspective of other individual programs in the system or from the perspective of the entire system.

There is a generally accepted set of ideas about how the workers' compensation program should be administered. Among the recurrent themes is the condemnation of compromise and release agreements as a method of terminating workers' compensation cases.[5] These agreements are often alleged to affect workers adversely because the settlement amounts are less than the benefits the workers would receive if payments were made on a periodic basis (Burton, Partridge, and Thomason 1986). In addition, the release component means that workers are unprotected if there are subsequent unanticipated medical or economic problems due to the work injuries.

Jerry Mashaw has drawn on his knowledge of the Social Security Disability Insurance program (SSDI) to identify the problems caused by the unavailability of compromise and release agreements (or their equivalents). Mashaw asserts that much of the reason for delay and litigation in the SSDI program is the inability to settle cases by compromise. Moreover, resolving cases by hearings often results in extreme variance in outcomes for similar cases, another problem that the ability to settle by compromise can help avoid.

Another of the shibboleths of workers' compensation that requires reexamination in light of Mashaw's contribution is the criticism of excessive litigation. Berkowitz and Burton, for example, recently asserted (1987, 384–85) that "as evidenced by the extent of litigation in most jurisdictions compared to Wisconsin, inefficiency seems to be

---

5. A compromise and release agreement, as defined by the national commission (1972, 109), "usually involves three elements: a compromise between the plaintiff's claim and the employer's previous offer concerning the amount of benefits to be paid; the payment of the compromised amount in a lump sum; and the release of the employer from further liability."

a serious problem" in workers' compensation. Mashaw argues that our reaction to increased use of the formal process of resolving cases is dependent on our view of the appropriate model of justice for the program. He describes the elements of three models and indicates that different levels of decision making in a program may rely on different models. He suggests that it may be appropriate for the appeals level of an agency to rely on an approach that is highly individualized and thus highly litigious. The cases most frequently contested in workers' compensation are permanent disability cases that must be resolved by use of "murky criteria"; such cases "one simply cannot expect to be adjudicated out of the system swiftly, correctly, and without dispute."

Lampman and Hutchens provide useful guidance for workers' compensation from the perspective of the entire workers' disability income system. Their data indicate the relative unimportance of workers' compensation, which accounted for only about 16 percent of all cash benefits for disability in 1982. The SSDI program by itself spends about 50 percent more than workers' compensation, even though that program is confined to totally disabled persons with extensive prior work experience.

Pointing out how small a share of disability benefits workers' compensation accounts for is not meant to denigrate the importance of the program but rather to alert us that the significance of these other programs must be considered in charting the future of workers' compensation. This means, as Larson says, that one of the tensions of the next decade will be the coordination of workers' compensation benefits with benefits from other public and private programs, including pensions. In those jurisdictions where workers' compensation benefits are now adequate, the combined total of those benefits and benefits from other programs that disabled workers may qualify for may be so high as to serve as a disincentive to work.

Another consequence of the relatively minor role of workers' compensation in the workers' disability income system is that increasingly policy makers are asking whether the policies used in the other parts of the system should be extended to workers' compensation. Some argue, for example, that workers' compensation benefits should be subject to federal income taxes, as is most of the cash income from private plans for disability.

Employers and policy makers are likely to raise an even more basic question: in light of the existence of all these other programs, why bother to differentiate work-related from other sources of disability? Many of the other programs in the system have much less litigation than workers' compensation, and arguably a solution to the extensive litigation in workers' compensation would be the elimination of the work-related test, perhaps by combining workers' compensation with the SSDI program, which does not require the disability to be work-related. Particularly since one of the primary rationales for the separate existence of workers' compensation—the promotion of workplace safety—has been seriously challenged in recent economic studies, the case for dismantling workers' compensation is increasingly persuasive.

Lampman and Hutchens review these arguments threatening the continued existence of workers' compensation and conclude that, for several reasons, the program is likely to survive for the foreseeable future. One reason is the disadvantages associated with alternative approaches to compensating work-related disabilities. The most litigious and expensive cases in workers' compensation involve compensation for permanent partial disabilities, and programs such as SSDI would have to be significantly restructured to deal with such cases. Another reason is that the medical benefits in workers' compensation are provided without deductibles or co-insurance and transferring responsibility for work-related injuries to another health care program (public or private) would probably require abandonment of these features. Lampman and Hutchens suggest that the major reason workers' compensation is likely to survive largely in its present form is the widely diffused political support for the program. They conclude that insofar as defenders of the program were able to ward off federal standards during the activist 1960s and 1970s, it is unlikely that new programs will take over the historic role of the states in workers' compensation.

National Developments with Implications for Workers' Compensation

There are a number of general developments in the country—economic, political, and legal—that are external to workers' compensation but that have implications for the future of the program.

The first development is the level of economic activity and, in particular, the condition of the labor market as reflected in the unemployment rate. Labor markets in recent years have been very slack. Indeed, the average unemployment rates for the 1970s and the 1980s are the worst in this century, except for the 1930s. One result of these high unemployment rates has been considerable pressures on all social insurance programs, including the Social Security program and workers' compensation. The programs are being used in part to take care of workers who cannot find jobs because of the interactions between adverse conditions in the labor market and personal characteristics such as age or physical handicaps. A study of New York's permanent partial disability benefits illustrates this (Burton 1983). During the 1970s, there was a rapid increase in the number and the cost of nonscheduled permanent partial benefits, and statistics indicate that about half the increases were due to the rise in the unemployment rate. What has happened in New York undoubtedly has happened in many other states.

The next decade is likely to have lower unemployment rates on average than the 1970s and 1980s. One of the most important reasons is that inflationary pressures, which were of such great concern during the 1970s, seem to have abated. This will make it easier to expand the economy and reduce unemployment without increasing inflation. A possible complication of this picture is the federal deficit, which so far has not caused a great deal of inflation but may as the economy moves closer to full employment. If the unemployment rate in the next decade is lower than in the past decade, workers' compensation is likely to benefit, because there will be less pressure on the program to take care of workers who are injured and cannot find jobs.

A second national development with implications for workers' compensation has to do with the changing demographic composition of the population. Over the next decade, the dependency ratio is going to decline. The dependency ratio is the sum of the number of persons younger than working age plus the workers who have already retired divided by the number of active workers. The decline over the next decade will make it easier for us to deal with some problems in the labor market, such as affording the payroll taxes for social insurance programs. Beginning about the year 2000, however, the number of older workers and the dependency ratio will go up very rapidly, leading to much higher payroll taxes. In the next decade, our problem is not going to be the aging work force but, if anything, a shortage of entry-level workers. The number of younger workers entering the labor force will be going down, as it has for the last few years.

What are the consequences of changes in the composition of the labor force for workers' compensation? On the one hand, traumatic injuries are likely to decline in the 1990s, because it is younger workers who typically are involved in accidents resulting in fractures or amputations. That decline in traumatic injuries is, obviously, a plus. On the other hand, as the average age of the labor force increases over the next decade, the problems associated with the aging process are going to be more prevalent. Heart disease, back disorders, and other degenerative diseases will increase. It is more difficult to determine whether these conditions are work-related and the extent of the disability than it is for traumatic injuries.

The changing composition of the work force has another favorable implication, because younger workers typically have higher unemployment rates than do older workers. Daniel Mitchell (1985) estimates that as the work force ages over the next decade, the overall unemployment rate will decline by about half a percentage point, just from that change in age. This development should also reduce the utilization of workers' compensation benefits by workers who will be able to find employment in the tighter labor market.

Another aspect of the changing composition of the labor force concerns immigration. The United States is likely to have considerable immigration in the next decade, partly because of the shortage of young workers. Immigration causes severe problems for workers' compensation, especially when illegal immigrants working for firms that do not provide workers' compensation try to get benefits after they are injured. Another complication is that many immigrants do not speak English, which makes it difficult for administrators and others to deal with their claims.

A third national development with implications for workers' compensation is the changing industrial/occupational composition. There has already been a major shift from blue-collar manufacturing jobs to white-collar service workers. In 1959, about 21 percent of all jobs were in manufacturing and 20 percent were in the services. By 1995, the prediction is that 18 percent of the jobs will be in manufacturing and 25 percent in services (Mitchell 1985). One of the favorable consequences of the shift from manufacturing to services is a likely decline in injuries. Manufacturing traditionally has been one of the sectors of the economy with the highest injury rates. Mitchell (1985) estimates that between 1979 and 1995, the average annual injury rate will drop about half a percentage point (from its current rate of about 9 percent of the work force) just because of the decline in the number of workers in manufacturing.

A fourth national development with some implications for workers' compensation is the declining importance or power of the union movement. The share of the labor force that is organized is declining very rapidly in this country. As recently as 1955, one in three workers was organized. Now, about one in five is organized, and unless unions improve their organizing record, the share of the labor force that is organized is going to decline to about one in ten workers (Freeman and Medoff 1984). Unions have been one of the major forces for reform in the workers' compensation program, both at the state and national levels, and as they lose their strength, they will find it increasingly difficult to play that role.

The four national developments just discussed have some political implications. I draw these implications in part from a recent analysis by William Baroody (1985). One trend already noticeable is the increasing political influence of older persons. Currently, about 27 percent of the federal budget is devoted to persons over the age of sixty-five. The projection is that by the year 2025, that percentage will be about 50 percent. This increase is in part due to the tendency of older persons to be active politically and to the increasing number of them in the population. This trend toward increasing the allocation of resources to older persons will take place at the same time the nation is likely to continue making substantial expenditures on defense, regardless of the outcome of negotiations over arms control. There will also be considerable pressure to reduce the federal deficit, which appears likely to remain a concern for at least five years, given the current tax rates and expenditure levels. There is a general reluctance to deal with the deficit by increasing taxes, which places pressure on the expenditure side.

All of these developments—the increasing political power of older persons, the declining strength of unions, the federal deficits— are likely to have consequences for social insurance programs, including workers' compensation. Domestic programs, apart from the old-age component of Social Security, are going to be under considerable pressure to restrict the growth of benefits. Poverty programs for the nonaged are likely to suffer. The Aid to Families with Dependent Children Program (AFDC) has already suffered a decline in real expenditures per recipient (that is, expenditures adjusted for inflation) of about 35 percent over the last fifteen years. The last ten years have produced significant changes in the poverty rate. Poverty has virtually disappeared among persons over the age of sixty-five because of the liberalization of Social Security old-age and Supplemental Security Insurance benefits. At the same time, the poverty rate for children has gone up dramatically. These developments reflect, in part, the political influence of older persons.

There also is evidence of a decline or, at least, a slowdown in the growth of expenditures in workers' compensation. Social Security data indicate that the employers' costs of workers' compensation as a percentage of payroll dropped from $1.96 per $100.00 of payroll in 1980 to $1.66 in 1984—a rather substantial decline (Price 1986). My research shows that between 1978 and 1984, employer expenditures on workers' compensation insurance dropped from about 1.5 percent of payroll to 1.3 percent of payroll (Burton, Hunt, and Krueger 1985), although preliminary data indicate that after 1984 increases have occurred. The evidence thus suggests that we now are in an era when workers' compensation costs (measured as a share of payroll) are relatively stable.

Another consequence of these recent political and economic trends is that continuing efforts will be made to subject the benefits in social insurance programs to federal income taxes. The federal government is desperately searching for ways to increase revenue and reduce the deficit. Portions of the old-age benefits of Social Security have been taxable for several years, and all unemployment insurance benefits are also subject to federal taxation. Inevitably, there will be pressure to make workers' compensation benefits taxable. Indeed, the Reagan tax reform package in 1985 proposed taxing workers' compensation benefits, and the idea is certain to reemerge.

Another national development with implications for workers' compensation is the concern over health care costs. Health care expenditures have been one of the most rapidly growing segments of the economy and now account for more than 10 percent of the gross national product. Price increases for health care consistently have exceeded those of the overall consumer price index. What we are seeing, as a result, is a variety of efforts to reduce the price increases and the total expenditures for health care. One effort involves use of deductibles; that is, requiring individuals to pay the initial dollars of their own health care. There also is an increased use of co-insurance, in which individuals pay a percentage of the cost of medical care above the deductible. These cost-sharing arrangements are showing up not only in legislative proposals but also in recent collective bargaining contracts, which increasingly have made employees responsible for a larger portion of their own health care costs. There also are numerous efforts to limit fees charged by hospitals and by doctors.

These efforts at cost containment will inevitably spill over into workers' compensation, as they have to some degree already. Workers' compensation is vulnerable, in some ways, because of the efforts in other health care programs to get hospitals and doctors to reduce their costs. In some jurisdictions, workers' compensation may have become a deep pocket for these other programs because the cost-containment movement is not as strong in the program as elsewhere.

Efforts to contain costs, including efforts to institute co-insurance and deductibles, are likely to increase markedly in the next decade in workers' compensation. This move will conflict with the long tradition in workers' compensation that medical care is totally free for workers. But almost inevitably, policy makers are going to propose that insured workers pay for part of their own health care.

Although that may sound like a fairly radical idea, workers' compensation already uses co-insurance and deductibles for cash benefits. A waiting period for temporary total benefits is a form of deductible, and the replacement of only two-thirds of lost wages is a form of co-insurance. There is nothing sacrosanct about bans on deductibles and co-insurance, although if such cost-containment devices were adopted for health care, offsetting adjustments in cash benefits might be appropriate.

Conclusions

This chapter has introduced several new perspectives on workers' compensation that should be not only of intellectual interest but of practical value. Those concerned with the program can increase their influence over its fate by recognizing the variety of influences that will affect the program in the next decade.

Some of the developments in the economy and society are beyond our control, but policy makers within workers' compensation can guide the program's response to them. For example, the national concern over health care costs has led to a number of cost-containment efforts in a variety of medical programs. If policy makers in workers' compensation are passive in light of these changes elsewhere, the program is likely to be increasingly saddled with costs that are marginally related to work injuries.

Viewing workers' compensation from the perspective of the workers' disability income system and other social insurance programs, such as Social Security, also has considerable value. The movement toward taxation of cash benefits in these programs should alert workers' compensation supporters that taxation schemes will also be proposed for workers' compensation, whether they are appropriate or not. Defenders of workers' compensation need to point out that the program has the spendable earnings concept as a basis for benefits. This concept, which was proposed by the national commission in 1972 and subsequently adopted in several states, provides a substitute for one of the primary virtues of taxing benefits, the elimination of the disincentive to return to work that results when untaxed benefits based on gross earnings exceed the worker's potential take-home pay.

Even within the workers' compensation program, new perspectives on old ideas can be helpful. If, for example, experience rating does not promote safety or health—as several recent economic studies have suggested—then designers of workers' compensation programs need to rethink the structure of the experience-rating plans or find other ways to achieve safe and healthful workplaces.

The ultimate conclusion is that a clear understanding of workers' compensation and of the forces that will shape its future requires familiarity with the several perspectives from which the program can be viewed. This volume is designed to help those concerned with the future of the program achieve that broad perspective.

2·TENSIONS OF THE NEXT DECADE

Arthur Larson

An often-heard criticism of military planners is that the generals always seem to be fighting not the next war, but the last war. In an area as swiftly changing as today's workers' compensation, we must be alert to the danger of deserving the same criticism, for the significant tensions of the next decade are going to be quite different from those of the last decade.

The story in the last decade has been largely one of bringing internal statutory standards on benefits and coverage up to those of the 1972 Report of the National Commission on State Workmen's Compensation Laws. This process, although by no means complete in some states,[1] has been remarkably successful. For example, in 1972, the unweighted average weekly maximum benefit for temporary total disability was $72. In July 1987, it was $331. In 1972, only fourteen states had automatic escalation provisions to keep benefit levels in line with wage levels. In 1986, forty-two states had such provisions. Moreover, all states now have, as a matter of statutory word-

---

1. There is always a danger, when one adduces evidence of improvement, of being thought insensitive to the deficiencies still to be corrected. It is true that the maximum weekly benefit is still too low in some states. A half-dozen still do not pay total permanent benefits for life. Too many workers, such as those in small firms in a few states, are still deprived of coverage. But the post-1972 improvement, when compared with the glacial movement of compensation change in any comparable pre-1972 period, fully deserves the adjective "remarkable."

ing,[2] full coverage of occupational diseases and unlimited medical benefits.

The national commission was central to this process in two ways. First, it provided a clear set of essential recommendations, backed by a respected and diverse body. Second, it supplied, through the threat of federal standards, a cogent incentive for compliance with the recommendations.

The important new fact of life, then, which more than any other development is responsible for the difference between the issues of the last decade and those of the next, is that for the first time in the history of workers' compensation, the main struggle for amelioration *does not* take the form of a never-ending battle to push benefits and coverage standards to a higher level. In the past, the larger part of the efforts of those striving to improve compensation went into tedious tussles every year or two over a $3 or $5 raise in the weekly benefit. Except in a few states, this is all behind us. Benefit levels are generally adequate, and what is more, they are going to stay adequate effortlessly, because of automatic escalation.

Old habits of thought and rhetoric are hard to shake, however. Well-intentioned champions of workers' compensation became, in some instances, so accustomed to talking about those miserable, stingy, starvation-level compensation benefits when the maximum was $50 that they keep on talking that way when it is $300. This is not mere harmless talk. Bad policy judgments that might have been innocuous in the $50 era become downright dangerous in the $300 era. Is your policy question whether duplication of benefits is harmful? Forty years ago the worker who got both Social Security and compensation benefits for the same week still had barely enough to live on, and judges and legislators could wink at overlapping benefits. Now that worker would in almost every case get more than his or her actual wage. Is your question whether a few holes should be punched in the exclusiveness-of-remedy doctrine? A judge who thought that the result would only help undo the severe inadequacy of compensation might, consciously or unconsciously, be influenced by this knowledge, leaving

---

2. Here again a caveat is in order: nominal full coverage on the face of the statute does not always mean fully satisfactory benefits in practice, as when "occupational disease" is too narrowly defined or high-quality medical care cannot be obtained within the rates set by regulation.

inroads into exclusiveness that are totally inexcusable in an era of adequate benefits.

What, then, will the tensions of the next decade be? At this point, one can detect four: the compensation-tort tension, especially as it relates to exclusiveness; the tension between income insurance and physical impairment payment; the new phase of the duplication problem, which involves drawing private plans within the coordination orbit; and the new form of federal-state tension, related primarily to occupational disease.

The Compensation-Tort Tension: Exclusiveness

The exclusiveness of the compensation remedy is a universal feature of American compensation law. It lies at the heart of the well-known quid pro quo, under which the employer enjoys tort immunity in exchange for accepting absolute liability for all work-connected injuries. The last state to give employees an option to sue employers in tort, New Hampshire, abolished that option in 1947. Since then, no frontal assault of any seriousness has been made on the exclusiveness principle in this country.

In recent years, however, selective attacks have been made on exclusiveness, and the trend for a time seemed to be toward a breakdown of exclusiveness. For years, a staple item on the program of workers' compensation conventions was "the erosion of exclusivity." Most recently, however, this trend has been not only halted but reversed. That favorite theme is no longer as prominent on convention programs. Here again, a major reason for its disappearance has undoubtedly been the improvement in compensation benefits. One must hasten to add, however, that this does not mean that there has been any letup in the vigor, variety, and ingenuity of attacks on exclusiveness. It means only that, in spite of these unending attempts, the final result, because of either judicial or legislative action, is that the doctrine of exclusiveness is in better health today than it was a few years ago. The following discussion of attacks on exclusiveness bolsters this somewhat surprising conclusion.

There have been six main lines of attack on exclusiveness: (1) nonphysical torts; (2) the dual-capacity doctrine; (3) the insurer as suable third party, for negligent safety inspection or medical treatment; (4) suits against co-employees, including physicians and corporate officers; (5) attempts to stretch the concept of "intentional" injury to include willful and wanton negligence; and (6) recovery-over by third parties against the employer for contribution or implied indemnity.

Nonphysical Torts

The five principal nonphysical torts that have figured in reported cases are false imprisonment, defamation, deceit, intentional infliction of emotional distress, and retaliation. Of these, the first two are of no great importance.

False imprisonment. The typical case here is that of a store manager who mistakenly holds an employee and grills him or her about a theft. Four or five such cases can be found in the reports, including, for example, *Smith v. Rich's, Inc.,*[3] which sustained such a suit. The basic test is usually whether the *essence* of the tort was nonphysical—even if perhaps some allegations of physical effects may have been made as makeweights.

Defamation. One of the rare examples here is *Braman v. Walthall.*[4] Although some illness was alleged as a consequence, the court permitted a suit in this case in which an employer called his store employees "lying thieves."

Deceit. Deceit is emerging as an extremely important category, because it is the principal vehicle for asbestos, byssinosis, uranium, and similar suits against an employer. The key here is to distinguish a single injury from a dual injury.

In the single-injury cases, the employer deceives the employee as to the hazards of the job, such as chemicals, fibers, and dusts, and the employee is injured as a result. This kind of action is almost universally held barred, because the deceit merges into the compensable injury itself. *Johnson v. Kerr-McGee Oil Industries, Inc.,*[5] for example, follows the present dual-injury analysis in holding that an

---

3. 104 Ga. App. 883, 123 S.E.2d 316 (1961).
4. 215 Ark. 582, 225 S.W.2d 342 (1949).
5. 631 P.2d 548 (Ariz. Ct. App. 1981).

action for tort would not lie for failure to warn the employee of the hazards to which he would be exposed in mining uranium.

Dual injury occurs when the employer deceives an employee after the employee has already incurred a work-connected injury, with the result that the employee suffers a second, additional or aggravated harm. An early case establishing the principle was *Ramey v. General Petroleum Corp.*[6] The employee charged that the employer and carrier had conspired to conceal the existence of the employee's cause of action against a third party with which the employer had a hold-harmless agreement. The statute ran, and the cause of action was destroyed. An action in deceit was held to lie.

The leading case applying the two-injury technique to asbestos-related cases is *Johns-Manville Products Co. v. Contra Costa Superior Court (Rudkin).*[7] Here the court held that, although an action would not lie against the employer for the consequences of the original failure to warn of asbestos hazards, an action would lie for deceiving employees as to their condition after the impact of asbestos exposure was known and thus depriving them of the opportunity to take appropriate steps to avoid further injury and to treat the illness promptly. This doctrine received important support in 1985 when the Supreme Court of New Jersey, on similar facts, reached a similar conclusion.[8] This dual-injury analysis is not, however, universally accepted. *Rivers v. New York Jets,*[9] for example, dismisses a suit against the employer for failing to inform the plaintiff football player of the true nature of his injuries.

Intentional infliction of emotional distress. A case whose melodramatic facts helped to popularize this cause of action was *Unruh v. Truck Insurance Exchange.*[10] The carrier, suspecting employees of malingering, sent a team of two investigators to get evidence for its suspicions. One got the female plaintiff emotionally involved with him. The other clandestinely photographed their activities, including her negotiating barrel bridges and the like at Disneyland in a fashion inconsistent with continued back disability. The shock of this revelation in the

---

6. 173 Cal. App. 2d 386, 343 P.2d 787 (1950).
7. 27 Cal. 3d 465, 165 Cal. Rptr. 858, 612 P.2d 948 (1980).
8. Millison v. E.I. duPont de Nemours & Co., 101 N.J. 161, 501 A.2d 505 (1985).
9. 460 F. Supp. 1233 (E.D. Mo. 1978), applying New York law.
10. 7 Cal. 3d 616, 102 Cal. Rptr. 815, 498 P.2d 1063 (1972).

hearing room caused the plaintiff to suffer a violent emotional collapse, leading to protracted hospitalization. A cause of action was held to lie against the carrier, free of the exclusiveness bar.

In that picturesque situations like this are not very common, this category would perhaps deserve little attention were it confined to comparable acts of treachery by insurance carriers. But when the underlying principle is extended to deliberate delay or terminations of payments by carriers, the potential importance of the principle becomes painfully clear. The first major case to make this extension was *Stafford v. Westchester Fire Insurance Co.*,[11] involving an aggravated set of facts showing deliberate delay and harassment by the carrier. An action was held to lie. A rash of similar attempts followed. In several extreme cases, *Stafford* was followed. But the significant fact for these purposes is that in most subsequent cases[12] the courts rejected the cause of action, seeing the danger of this development as an open-ended invitation to sue in tort for any delay in payment, merely by calling it intentional infliction of emotional distress, or "outrage," or some such term.

Retaliation. The first case to hold retaliatory discharge for filing a compensation claim actionable was the Indiana Supreme Court decision in *Frampton v. Central Indiana Gas Co.*[13] The ground was the public policy exception to the exployment-at-will doctrine. Most courts have followed *Frampton*, including those of California, Illinois, Michigan, New Jersey, and Oregon. In addition, a number of jurisdictions have nonretaliation statutes: the Longshoremen's Act and those of Arizona (in its constitution), California, Hawaii, Maine, Maryland, Michigan, Missouri, New Jersey, New York, North Carolina, Ohio, Oklahoma, Texas, and Wisconsin. Several states, however, still cling to the absolute employment-at-will doctrine: Alabama, Mississippi, and New Mexico. This minority view must be regarded as distinctly anachronistic. In time, remedies for retaliatory discharge will no doubt become routine.[14] After all, consider the alternative. The state says

---

11. 526 P.2d 37 (Alaska 1974).
12. *See, e.g.,* Sullivan v. Liberty Mutual Ins. Co., 367 So. 2d 658 (Fla. App. 1979).
13. 297 N.E.2d 425 (Ind. 1973).
14. In late 1985, South Carolina recognized the public policy exception to employment-at-will in another context. Ludwick v. This Minute of Carolina, 321 S.E.2d

to the worker: "The community has decided that when you are injured you shall receive compensation benefits." The employer says to the worker: "Oh, no, you don't, because *I* have decided that you shall *not* receive compensation benefits—and if you ask for them you're fired." Which is to prevail—the employer's policy or the state's?

The Dual-Capacity Doctrine

The dual-capacity doctrine is well illustrated by a case from Ohio, one of the only two jurisdictions in which the doctrine once flourished. In *Mercer v. Uniroyal, Inc.*[15] a truck driver who was injured when a tire blew out discovered that the tire had been manufactured by his employer and sued the employer in products liability. The Ohio court held that the action was not barred because the employer was being sued in its second capacity as a products manufacturer. It is unnecessary to belabor the obvious fallacies of this holding. What is most relevant here is the number of jurisdictions in which a similar dual-capacity approach has been attempted and rejected. As of mid-1987, the doctrine had been expressly rejected in more than thirty jurisdictions. The most popular category remains that of products liability. The next most popular is the suit against the employer as owner or occupier of land, in which the rejection of the doctrine is unanimous. Another prolific area is that of employers, either public or private, that have separate operating divisions or departments. A typical case is that of a city that has both a fire department and a street railway line. The widow of a fireman killed as a result of negligence by the street railway could not maintain an action against the city in its capacity as street railway operator.[16] Here again the rule is universal.

Finally, there is the effort to sue the employer for malpractice by the company doctor, on the theory that the employer's capacity is somehow separate when it becomes a provider of medical services.

---

618 (S.C. Ct. App. 1984), *rev'd*, No. 22408 (S.C. Nov. 18, 1985). *See* LARSON, UNJUST DISMISSAL, §10.42[2].

15. 49 Ohio App. 2d 279, 361 N.E.2d 492 (1977).

16. Walker v. City and County of San Francisco, 97 Cal. App. 2d 901, 219 P.2d 487 (1950).

The leading case rejecting this idea was the Illinois Supreme Court's decision in *McCormick v. Caterpillar Tractor Co.*,[17] which based its decision on the simple ground that the employer as employer was required by law to furnish the medical services—and so the employer could hardly be said to be someone other than the employer while discharging that duty.

The Supreme Court of Ohio in 1983 went a long way toward destroying the doctrine by adopting my recommendation that a separate legal persona be required.[18] California, whose courts had run the doctrine into the ground even more enthusiastically than had Ohio's, abolished it by a 1982 statutory amendment.[19] It is poignant to reflect that California has thus exchanged the distinction of being the most permissive state on this doctrine for that of being the most restrictive. This is because the amendment makes no allowance for the occasional rare case in which recognition of a separate suable legal persona would be legitimate, as might happen in the case, for example, of a trustee or guardian.

Insurer as Suable Third Party

This is another example of a segment of the law of exclusiveness that at one time appeared to be headed in the direction of a major demolition of carrier immunity and that, as the result of reactions by both courts and legislatures, has largely reversed itself. The case that caused the greatest consternation in the carrier community was the *Nelson v. Union Wire Rope Corp.* decision.[20] The carrier had allegedly been negligent in its voluntary inspection of an elevator cable, as a result of which an elevator fell and several workers were killed. The Illinois Supreme Court, applying the Florida compensation act, held that an action would lie.

Twenty years later, a rough count of jurisdictions that have dealt with this matter reveals that carriers may be held liable for negligent inspections or negligent medical care in only seven states and are immune in twenty. Compared with the crisis atmosphere and

---

17. Ill. 2d 352, 423 N.E.2d 876 (1981).
18. Freese v. Consolidated Rail Corp., 3 Ohio St. 3d 5, 445 N.E.2d 1110 (1983).
19. Assembly Bill No. 684 § 6 (1982) (amending § 3602 of the Labor Code).
20. 31 Ill. 2d 69, 199 N.E.2d 769 (1968).

frantic activity following *Wire Rope*, this threat to carrier immunity seems to have largely faded as a major issue.

Co-employees as Third Parties

About ten years ago, co-employees were liable to suit as third parties in two-thirds of the states. Now they are immune to suit in two-thirds of the states. One can only speculate on the reason for this burst of legislative activity, but it is probably due in considerable measure to the coinciding of parking lot accidents with the spread of mandatory liability insurance that made suits against co-employees worthwhile.

Moreover, corporate officers are generally held immune as co-employees. Thus, Michigan has even included within the term "a natural person in the same employ" the president, manager, and sole stockholder of a corporation.[21]

Stretching "Intentional" Injury

All states have eventually resisted the effort to stretch the concept of "intentional" injury, which is often made an exception to employer immunity, to include willful, wanton, gross, or other aggravated negligence or misconduct short of genuine intent to inflict bodily injury. For a time there were two out-of-line states, West Virginia in its *Mandolides v. Elkins Industries, Inc.*, case[22] and Ohio in its *Blankenship v. Cincinnati-Milacron Chemicals* opinion.[23] Then, just as happened with dual capacity in California, the West Virginia legislature in 1983 in effect overruled *Mandolides*, leaving Ohio once more in lonely isolation. The isolation ended in 1986, when the Ohio legislature amended the statute to undo *Blankenship* and a series of later cases that had carried the *Blankenship* rule to almost every possible extreme.

The next state to start down this treacherous path was Michigan. Fully conscious of what had happened in Ohio, and avowedly determined not to fall into the same morass, the Michigan Supreme Court in *Beauchamp v. Dow Chemical Co.*[24] adopted what it evidently thought was a moderate compromise. It held that an intentional tort

---

21. Pettaway v. McConaghy, 367 Mich. 651, 116 N.W.2d 789 (1962).
22. 246 S.E.2d 907 (W. Va. 1978), in effect overruled by W. Va. H.B. 1201.
23. 69 Ohio St. 608, 433 N.E.2d 572 (1982).
24. 427 Mich. 1, 398 N.W.2d 882 (1986).

was not banned under the exclusiveness doctrine, and then went on to define "intention" to include any injury in which the employer intended the act itself and also believed that the injurious consequence was "substantially certain" to occur.

If the court had paid more attention to what had been happening in Louisiana, it might have realized that the flaw in this definition was not a conceptual one; it was the demonstrated practical danger that through the chink of "substantially certain" such a flood of exceptions to exclusiveness would rush as to threaten to destroy the defense altogether. In Louisiana, the problem began with what seemed to be a sensible exposition of the intentional tort exception in *Bazley v. Tortorich*.[25] But later Louisiana courts extracted from the opinion the term "substantially certain" and have used it, not always successfully of course, to litter the reports with situations for which "preposterous" would be too charitable a term. One example, the handiwork of the Louisiana Supreme Court itself, should suffice to justify this severe criticism. In *Mayer v. Valentine Sugars, Inc.*,[26] the court solemnly concluded that the employer intentionally blew up his own plant for the purpose of injuring his employees.

The Michigan legislature evidently decided not to wait to see whether the West Virginia–Ohio–Louisiana story would play itself out in Michigan. It promptly overruled *Beauchamp* by a legislative amendment in early 1987.

What is most significant, however, is not so much that two or three states have temporarily deviated from the "intent means intent" standard as that, in spite of a constant barrage of assaults on this line, at least thirty-three jurisdictions have expressly rebuffed the attempt. This result is the more remarkable in that the alleged conduct in some of these cases goes beyond mere aggravated negligence. Thus the deliberate sealing or removal of safety guards from machines has been repeatedly held to fall short of deliberate intent to injure.[27]

A very recent development, the use of criminal prosecutions of employers, should be mentioned here, for it may supply a partial answer to the indignation that is felt when employers are shielded from tort suits in extreme cases. The best-known case, *People v. Film*

25. 397 So. 2d 475 (La. 1981).
26. 444 So. 2d 618 (La. 1984).
27. Artonio v. Hirsh, 3 A.D.2d 939, 163 N.Y.S.2d 489 (1957).

Recovery Systems,[28] involved an employer who was in the business of recovering silver from film negatives. The negatives were placed in vats of cyanide, from which cyanide gas would bubble up in an inadequately ventilated workplace. The employer knew all about the danger. Because the labels on the chemicals contained adequate warnings, the employer hired only employees who could not read or speak English. The workers complained daily about the fumes. In 1981 an inspector warned the employer that the operation had outgrown the plant. The employer's response was to triple the size of the operation but move the executive offices. Eventually one worker died and several were seriously injured as the result of cyanide poisoning. The corporate officers were convicted of involuntary manslaughter and sentenced to twenty-five-year prison terms. They were also fined $10,000 each on the involuntary manslaughter count and $1,000 for each of fourteen counts of reckless conduct.

Reports of similar activity are beginning to come in from all parts of the country: thirteen indictments for criminally negligent homicide have been obtained in Austin, Texas, following the deaths of three workers in trenching accidents; a special group, including a "roll-out unit," has been established by the Los Angeles County District Attorney to investigate fatal workplace accidents, and criminal charges have been lodged in two cases; and a Seattle construction firm in another trenching case was fined $10,000 and went out of business.

Recovery-Over by Third Parties against Employers

Unlike the first five lines of attacks on exclusiveness, recovery-over by third parties against employers involves an indirect rather than a direct invasion of the employer's immunity, but it may well be the most serious of all. In the typical situation, a worker who has been injured by a defective machine recovers damages from the machine manufacturer in products liability. The manufacturer, in turn, brings an action against the employer, alleging that the employer had removed the guards from the machine and otherwise tampered with it. The employer, of course, defends against the claim for contribution or indemnity on the ground that compensation liability is exclusive.

---

28. Cited by the *Beauchamp* court, *supra* note 24, 398 N.W.2d at 892.

When my workers' compensation treatise was published in 1953, the discussion of this problem began with the statement that this is "the most evenly-balanced controversy in all of compensation law."[29] This is the most-quoted passage in the treatise, and the statement is as true as it ever was.

The principal point here is that the classical rule barring both contribution and indemnity is still the clear majority rule and indeed has gained ground in recent years. This may come as a surprise to some, because most of the headlines have been about a handful of unorthodox and uninhibited *contra* decisions. New York, in *Dole v. Dow Chemical Co.*,[30] held that a third party can recover from a negligent employer in indemnity an amount proportional to the employer's share of fault. Minnesota, in *Lambertson v. Cincinnati Corp.*,[31] allowed contribution in proportion to fault, but in no event beyond the employer's compensation liability. Illinois, in *Skinner v. Reed-Prentice Division*,[32] allowed contribution in proportion to the employer's fault without limit.

These showy developments are, however, outweighed by such countervailing events as the legislative reversal by Congress in 1972 of the *Ryan Stevedoring Co. v. Pan-Atlantic S.S. Corp.*[33] doctrine, which dominated this area of law for most of its existence; the restoration of the classical rule in Pennsylvania by legislative action in 1974;[34] and the quiet but relentless bolstering of the majority rule during this same period by judicial decisions in such key states as New Jersey,[35] Texas,[36] and Michigan.[37]

Nevertheless, there will undoubtedly continue to be both legislative and judicial attempts to contrive a compromise solution. One rather drastic proposal, which has enjoyed a surprising degree of support,[38] would in *all* cases reduce the employee's third-party re-

---

29. Larson (1953), § 76.11 at n.1.
30. 30 N.Y.2d 143, 282 N.E.2d 288, 331 N.Y.S.2d 382 (1972).
31. 312 Minn. 114, 257 N.W.2d 679 (1977).
32. 70 Ill. 2d 1, 374 N.E.2d 437 (1978).
33. 350 U.S. 124 (1956).
34. Pa. Cons. Stat. § 303(b) (1974).
35. Schweizer v. Elox Div. of Colt Indus., 70 N.J. 280, 359 A.2d 857 (1976). Ruvolo v. United States Steel Corp., 179 N.J. Super. 578, 354 A.2d 685 (1976).
36. Grove Mfg. Co. v. Cardinal Constr. Co., 534 S.W.2d 153 (Tex. Civ. App. 1976).
37. Langley v. Harris Corp., 413 Mich. 592, 321 N.W.2d 662 (1982).
38. This plan has, in effect, been endorsed by the American Insurance As-

covery by the amount of his or her compensation; abolish the employer's right of subrogation against the third party; and abolish, where it existed, any right of recovery-over by the third party against the employer. The idea is that the employee would come out whole in any event and that the gains and losses between the employer and the third party and particularly their insurers would eventually cancel out. The appeal of this idea lies in its simplicity. There would be one cause of action and one recovery, no more. It should never be forgotten that simplicity and elimination of litigation are, after all, prime objectives of the original workers' compensation legislation.

Balance Sheet on Exclusiveness

What are the gains and losses of exclusiveness? Is the doctrine of exclusiveness indeed in better health today than it was a few years ago?

Nonphysical torts. The line has generally been held on rejecting actions for deceit as to original harmful exposure. The initial trend to allow tort actions for delayed payments by carriers has been checked and reversed.

Dual capacity. The adoption of the California amendment and of the legal persona doctrine in Ohio leaves no state in which the dual-capacity doctrine is generally accepted.

Insurers as third parties. The score, after a preliminary burst of cases finding suability, is now twenty to seven for immunity.

Co-employee immunity. The score has changed from two to one denying immunity to two to one granting it.

Stretching "intentional." Following the West Virginia amendment and the Ohio amendments, there is now no state that accepts gross negligence as intention.

Third party's recovery-over against the employer. The classical rule respecting the employer's immunity has on the whole been gaining strength, although a few courts have dramatically broken ranks.

---

sociation, in *Product Liability Legislative Package*, March 1977, and by the American Bar Association Special Committee to Study Product Liability, *Report to the House of Delegates*, February 1983, and has been incorporated in the Kasten "Product Liability Bill," S. 44, 98th Cong. 1st Sess. § 11 (1984). It has also been enacted by Connecticut, PA79-483.

Tension between Income Insurance and Physical Impairment Payment

The most damaging single trend in the modern compensation story has been the imperceptible shift, in many states, away from protection against actual income loss as the central function of the system and toward cash payment for physical impairment. The reaction against this trend, involving a campaign to restore to primacy the traditional function of preventing real destitution that results from interruption of earnings, has come to be known as the "wage-loss movement." It is strongly associated with the Florida amendments of 1979. Louisiana, Saskatchewan, New Brunswick, Newfoundland, the Yukon, and Quebec have also enacted wage-loss reforms, and a number of states and provinces have plans under study.

There is every reason to anticipate that, in spite of opposition from the trial bar and sometimes from organized labor, the pressure for such reform will continue to mount during the coming decade. The main reason is that compensation costs have soared so high that they presumably cannot be pushed much higher, and, at the same time, the wage-loss approach offers the only solution that can demonstrably cut costs while doing a better job of providing the protection that is the system's real reason for existence.

It is clear that, on the whole, the Florida reforms are succeeding in achieving the improvements that had been hoped for. Litigation has been reduced; total claims have been sharply cut, and the great majority of these have been disposed of without hearings; legal costs and insurance rates have decreased; and general surveys show that claimants are satisfied with the system.

It is also clear, however, that a "pure" wage-loss system, meaning one that abolishes the schedule altogether, is not a politically realistic possibility anywhere. It has become obvious that the issue is not whether the overblown schedule systems in some states can be completely eliminated, but rather whether they can be replaced by a schedule so carefully limited as to retain the basic advantages of a wage-loss approach. This might be called the Saskatchewan pattern.

The key feature of this pattern is that it does not pretend to make the schedule a substitute for a wage-loss award, based on a conclusive presumption of wage loss. Rather, it superimposes on the wage-loss income benefit a modest cash supplement that is frankly designed to compensate for a claimant's losses in private life because of his or her impairment. Consistent with this theory, the award is for a flat amount unrelated to prior earnings. Moreover, the limitation of the range of schedule items largely avoids the principal defect in systems that overemphasize the schedule—the waste of administrative, judicial, legal, and medical time that goes into quibbling over evaluations of disabilities.

A further lesson to be drawn from Florida's experience is that, to operate efficiently and fairly, a wage-loss system depends, in general, on high-quality administration and, in particular, on a working solution to the problem of identifying which periods of wage loss, after the initial obvious period following the injury, are work-related. Suppose a worker, although still retaining some of the effects of an injury, recovers sufficiently to resume his or her old job—say, for six months. Suppose he or she is then fired for misconduct, or is laid off in a general reduction in force, or quits to take a better job that falls through. Suppose that at this point he or she is unable to get another job because of the lingering effects of the injury. Is this subsequent period of unemployment work-related? Florida wrestled with this problem for years, both legislatively and judicially, and still has not achieved a well-balanced solution. Any state that is disposed to adopt a wage-loss statute would do well to meet this problem in advance, by writing a few simple rules into the statute itself. The key is to recognize that a clear distinction must be observed between the initial work search immediately following recovery and a subsequent work search following a period of some employment.

The following notes for such a statutory solution are offered for the guidance of any draftsman approaching this problem.

1. As to the initial work search, the claimant must only prove
(a) a continuing work-connected physical (or mental) disability;
(b) a suitable work search;
(c) inability to get a suitable job.

It is important to note that the claimant need *not* prove that the inability was due to physical causes; on the first work search, this is presumed. Nor need the claimant prove that he or she has revealed the disability to prospective employers; this is an unrealistic impediment to getting the first postinjury job. A further condition is that the employer can defend on only two grounds: no physical disability or inadequate work search. He *cannot* defend on the ground that failure to find work was for economic reasons.

2. As to subsequent unemployment, after the claimant has held a regular job (not necessarily the same as the old job), with comparable wage, and *not* in any degree a sheltered or make-work job:

(a) claimant must first prove the same two initial elements: disability and work search and rejection.

(b) the burden is then on the employer to show that the cause was economic (or other—e.g., misconduct) and that a person without the disability would also be unemployed.

(c) the claimant can then rebut this defense by proving that the nature of the disability is such that it would, in the perception of an average employer, place him or her at a disadvantage in obtaining and holding employment relative to a worker without the disability—even under the adverse economic conditions, i.e., the disabled person, although a lot of able-bodied people are fired in slack times, is the first fired and the last rehired.

Coordination of Income-Protection Systems

The accelerating need for coordination of all income-protection systems, both public and private, is, once more, strongly related to the general increase in benefit levels.

The biggest part of the coordination job was accomplished when the Social Security offset provision was adopted—but this did not occur without a considerable struggle. When disability benefits were first added to the Social Security Act in 1956, a rather crude offset provision was included. In 1958 this provision was quietly repealed, and it took until 1965 to get it replaced with the present version, which states that the Social Security disability benefit for any month shall be reduced to the point at which the combined Social Security and periodic compensation benefit does not exceed 80 percent of the individual's average preinjury earnings.

A comparatively recent development was the appearance of

state deductions in compensation benefits for Social Security benefits. Sixteen states have some such offset.[39]

It may seem odd, considering the intense concern about compensation costs, that the states were so slow to exploit this obvious way to reduce their compensation burden. Although the federal offset in its current form was enacted in 1965, thus ensuring that there would be a ceiling on the combined benefits and that the federal Social Security program would reap all the savings from the elimination of overlap, by 1975—ten years later—only three states had countered with offset provisions of their own: Colorado, Montana, and Minnesota. The number rather rapidly grew to sixteen, but more than two-thirds of the states were still forgoing this cost-cutting opportunity. Then the federal government, realizing that the states were beginning to shift part of their compensation burden to the Social Security system, enacted legislation effectively ruling out any future adoption of offsets at the state end.[40]

To understand this remarkable display of generosity toward the federal government on the part of two-thirds of the states, one must reconstruct the sometimes almost irrational fear of federalization that has permeated the compensation community for many years. When I presided over the drafting of the Council of State Governments Model Act, the question of an offset to prevent combined benefits from exceeding wages was much discussed. The federal offset proposal was pending, and I suggested to the committee that we write a state offset into the model act. This recommendation met with unanimous opposition. The most vigorous opposition came from the representative of the United States Chamber of Commerce. Finally I asked him point-blank, "Would you rather have a state offset or pay duplicate benefits?" The answer came back unhesitatingly: "I would rather pay duplicate benefits." Applying a state offset was viewed as a pro tanto abdication of a portion of state workers' compensation to the federal government, and even this relatively minor bit of "federalization" appeared so threatening that overlapping benefits were not too high a price to pay to avoid it.

---

39. Alaska, California, Colorado, Florida, Louisiana, Michigan, Minnesota, Montana, New Hampshire, New Jersey, New York, North Dakota, Oregon, Utah, Washington, and Wisconsin. Saskatchewan and six other Canadian provinces have similar offsets.

40. Pub. L. No. 97-35 (1981) (amending 42 U.S.C. §424(a)).

As to unemployment compensation, although the majority of unemployment insurance statutes specifically forbid benefits to anyone drawing workers' compensation, only eight workers' compensation statutes contain any offset for unemployment insurance benefits.[41] In the absence of such a statutory offset, most states that have dealt with the problem have held that there is no inherent reason why a person drawing unemployment benefits cannot also receive workers' compensation benefits. Clearly this is an area that requires attention. The obvious solution is a legislative amendment, and there are adequate models to choose from.

The most sensitive area of all, however, is that of private pensions provided by the employer or union or both. Under the original British act, the result in the case of pensions unilaterally supplied by the employer was a deduction, because of the statutory admonition that, in fixing the compensation payable, regard should be had to any "payment, allowance, or benefit" received from the employer during the disability. For some reason, American states did not generally copy this offset provision, and it remains exceptional to this day. Only a handful of states, including Colorado, Ohio, Pennsylvania, California, Maine, and Michigan, achieve this coordination either directly or indirectly.[42]

One reason the area of private plans is so delicate is that employees take a more proprietary attitude toward private benefits than they do toward public plans. They will argue that they have, in effect, bought and paid for these benefits by accepting them in place of higher per-hour wages for which they might have bargained. This same attitude exists to some degree toward Social Security offsets, which is why many states limit the offsets to 50 percent, thus recognizing that the other 50 percent was bought with the claimant's own contribution. With private plans, however, the feeling runs even deeper, causing legislatures to hesitate to take this final step toward a properly coordinated total system. Whatever the merits of this conceptual argument, it is more than outweighed by the implacable ne-

---

41. Alaska, California, Florida, Louisiana, Maine, Massachusetts, Michigan, and Pennsylvania.

42. In Canada, coordination with private plans is the rule rather than the exception. The Saskatchewan provision is taken directly from the British. Since Canadian systems are financed by state funds, they may provide, as does Saskatchewan's, that the employer's outlay on the private plan may be refunded to the employer when compensation is payable out of the fund.

cessity of avoiding at all costs a situation in which it is more profitable to be disabled than well. In the last analysis, if a claimant's total benefit dollars when he or she is disabled exceed his or her total take-home dollars when he or she is working, the disincentive to return to work is just as great when some of the benefit dollars are from private plans as when they are all from public plans.

Federal-State Tension

One of the most conspicuous changes between the last decade and the next is the abrupt disappearance of the issue of mandatory federal standards. Only a few years ago this was the dominant topic at workers' compensation conferences, seminars, and conventions across the country. The imperfections of the current Williams-Javits bill were exposed and debated, and a year later a revised Williams-Javits bill would appear, only to be criticized in turn. This went on for some years. Then, overnight, there was no Williams-Javits bill to criticize. What happened? Several things. The central problem in drafting the bill—how to make federal standards mandatory without actually federalizing workers' compensation, which was politically unthinkable—was never solved. Various sanctions short of outright federalization were tried, but they were either ineffective or unconstitutional or both. Moreover, the bills were always top-heavy with nonessential standards, included to satisfy the untiring lobbyists for chiropractors, faith healers, and the like.

Undoubtedly, however, the principal reason for the disappearance of federal standards as the dominant issue was that all this time the states were raising their benefits and other standards to the point where there was eventually no longer any general need for federal standards. If those who labored so hard for federal-standards legislation want to take some satisfaction from the fact that the in terrorem effect of the federal threat was a major incentive to this improvement, they have every right to enjoy this consolation prize.

This does not mean, however, that we have seen the last of federal-state tension. The difference is that in the coming decade it will concern not across-the-board but selective federal involvement.

For some time now it has been thought that the prime target for selective federal involvement was occupational disease in general and asbestos-related diseases in particular. There were two main reasons for this view. One was the sheer magnitude of the crisis—more than twenty-five thousand claimants have filed asbestos-related lawsuits, and six thousand new cases are being filed every year. The other was the long latency period for these diseases. When diseases may take twenty to forty years after exposure to manifest themselves, the difficulty of identifying a claim with a particular state and a particular employer is formidable.

The result was a burst of proposed federal legislation, beginning in about 1980, that for variety and energy surpassed even the federal-standards effort. There was the Fenwick bill (H.R. 5224); the Hart bill (S.1643); the Miller bill (H.R. 5735), favored by organized labor; and a succession of industry bills, beginning with the Asbestos Workers' Recovery Act, or Percy bill (S.2708). The Fenwick and Hart bills bowed out early in the story. The Miller bill went through a number of changes, becoming the Williams bill (H.R. 3090) in 1985. This bill and the revised industry bill, which became the Armstrong bill (S.1265) and Murphy bill (H.R. 1626), were the subject of Senate committee hearings in 1985. Then, quite suddenly, as in the case of federal-standards legislation, there was nothing. In 1987 there was neither a labor nor an industry bill pending. Evidently both sides had become discouraged with the almost complete absence of real progress and had decided that their efforts could be better spent elsewhere. The industry has decided to "go back to square one" and is said to be examining a half-dozen new approaches to the problem. Some of the desperateness of the situation has been alleviated by the success of the voluntary Asbestos Claims Facility, by the $640 million settlement of the industry with the insurers, and by the plan pending in the Manville bankruptcy proceeding to sign over a percentage of profits to future claimants as a condition of release from bankruptcy.

The pressure for federal involvement in the occupational disease area has not, however, disappeared. It has merely shifted its focus to a new and apparently more promising target, the High Risk Occupational Disease Notification and Prevention Act.

In its original version, this bill (H.R. 1309), introduced by Congressman Joseph Gaydos, would have required employers to notify an employee of any disease that studies indicated occurred at a higher-than-normal rate in the particular employee population of which that employee was a member. The idea was to ensure early detection, monitoring, and treatment of disease. "Increased risk" was defined as incidence 30 percent greater than in the general public.

Although the goal of early detection of disease was generally conceded to be a laudable one, the breadth and looseness of the provisions of the bill caused widespread consternation in industry. After intensive negotiations, ten substantial changes were made, sufficient to win over at least a part of the business community. By August 1987, the revised House and Senate versions, which are essentially similar to each other, were ready for floor action as H.R. 162 (Gaydos) and S.79 (Metzenbaum). But the secretaries of labor, of health and human services, and of commerce, the attorney general, and the administrator of the Small Business Administration have jointly announced that they will recommend a veto if the bill is passed. By late spring of 1988, the bill was dead for that session, but no doubt it will be revived in the next.

The principal continuing objection to this legislation is that it would stimulate a flood of workers' compensation and tort claims. With the rapid spread of compensation awards in "stress cases,"[43] employers are concerned about the possibility that a worker, having been notified that he or she has been exposed to a cancer-producing substance and having had a nervous collapse from sheer worry about the possibility of getting cancer, will successfully claim compensation for that disability. Cases suggesting this possibility have already begun to appear in the reports. In the 1985 California case of *Cooper v. Workers' Compensation Appeals Board*,[44] the claimant had been exposed to asbestos in his work. When he was diagnosed—perhaps incorrectly—to have asbestosis, he suffered conversion hysteria with depression, although he was not in the least physically disabled. The board set aside an award, but the court restored it. It was not material whether the claimant in fact had asbestosis, since it was the medical diagnosis that precipitated the hysteria and since the medical diagnosis arose out of the employment. Substitute "notification of exposure" for "medical diagnosis," and the case fits the present problem.

New Mexico has also recognized the compensability of neurosis caused by exposure anxiety, in this case involving radiation. In *Mar-*

43. *See* LARSON, WORKMEN'S COMPENSATION, §42.25.
44. 173 Cal. App. 3d 44, 218 Cal. Rptr. 783 (1985).

tinez v. University of California,[45] the claimant's work as a foundry technician had entailed frequent exposure to radioactive materials. Coworkers had suffered fatal illnesses and cancers of unknown origin. After the claimant had a cancerous growth removed from his eye, he suffered extreme anxiety that eventually made him unable to continue work. He was diagnosed as having an anxiety neurosis, which manifested itself as a phobia concerning radioactive exposure. The New Mexico Supreme Court reversed the appeals court and granted the claim under New Mexico's Occupational Disease Disablement Law. Whether the claimant's neurosis was an occupational disease depended on whether there was a recognizable link between the disease and some distinctive feature of the claimant's job. The claimant's work involved an excessive hazard of radiation over a long period, and this fact, along with the unexplained illnesses of fellow workers, provided the recognizable causal link between the neurosis and the claimant's occupation.

Those members of the business community who have gone along with the revised bill have done so on the theory that some notification act would probably be passed and so the most prudent course was to settle for an acceptable moderate bill. Thus the current version contains no automatic 30 percent "trigger." The seven-member Risk Assessment Board must make specific surveys of what exposures are hazardous and which populations are at risk, based not on isolated animal studies but on human evidence and the epidemiology of particular plants. So exacting are the standards that some business and insurance representatives believe that, except for a handful of well-known toxic substances, it will be a long time before widespread notifications will occur—if they ever do.

The majority of business interests, however, still mistrust this legislation. A typical apprehension is that voiced by J. Eldred Hill, Jr., president of UBA, in his August 10, 1987, newsletter: "We remain convinced that this legislation would produce a flood of unmeritorious workers' compensation and tort claims. It would establish a new federal bureaucracy whose 'manifest' destiny would be jurisdiction over all occupational disease claims, including the compensation of those claims."

---

45. 601 P.2d 425 (N.M. 1979). *See also* McMahon v. Anaconda Co., 678 P.2d 661 (Mont. 1984).

This quotation may serve as a reminder that, at every point where the state-federal tension manifests itself, whether on across-the-board involvement or on increasingly specialized selective involvement, the one most potent and durable force is the implacable opposition of most of the workers' compensation community to any change that is seen to involve either a present or a potential threat of federal encroachment on the traditional state jurisdiction over workers' compensation.

Conclusion

These, then, appear to be the four principal areas of policy controversy for the next decade. There are, of course, many other ongoing issues, notably those involving the improvement of administration, which underlies the success of the system at every point. And, if the past is any guide, new crises may explode and dominate the scene for a time—crises that we cannot now predict.

The tensions we can now foresee have on the whole one heartening feature: if they are resolved wisely, the overall cost of compensating for industrial injury and disease can actually be lowered, while the quality of the job done by the system can be markedly improved.

3 PAYING FOR ASBESTOS-RELATED DISEASES UNDER WORKERS' COMPENSATION

Donald N. Dewees

Just as asbestos-related diseases have proven to be a nightmare for workers exposed to high concentrations of asbestos, so the growing torrent of claims from those workers has become a problem for the workers' compensation agencies and insurers that must deal with them. The volume of the claims, their cost, and their complexity creates burdens for state compensation funds and causes employers and insurers to resist with vigor all but the most meritorious of claims. The claims are especially difficult and costly to handle because of the long delay that frequently occurs between workplace exposure and the onset of a compensable disease. With respect to lung cancer, proving work-relatedness is impossible, so procedures must be adopted that compensate adequately without overcompensating. Often the participants in the compensation process feel they are not being dealt with fairly.

This chapter deals with three topics arising out of the study of

This research has been supported in part by a grant from the Social Sciences and Humanities Research Council of Canada and by a grant of computer time from the Department of Economics of the University of Toronto. The Gilbert White Fellowship of Resources for the Future has provided time and word processing services. I am grateful for this financial support. In addition, I would like to thank James E. Pesando and Michael Berkowitz for very considerable help in developing and evaluating the financial model summarized in this chapter. Sherry Glied provided invaluable research assistance and computer programming service.

workers' compensation by the Ontario Royal Commission on Matters of Health and Safety Arising from the Use of Asbestos in Ontario, commonly called the Ontario Royal Commission on Asbestos, or the RCA. The RCA spent four years and $1.7 million studying all aspects of the asbestos problem and devoted three chapters out of fifteen in its report (1984) to the problems of workers' compensation. In parts, this chapter borrows from the text of the RCA report, while elsewhere it goes beyond the report. This chapter considers first the measurement of the degree of impairment for progressive diseases, specifically asbestosis. It then discusses the financing of workers' compensation claims arising from asbestos exposure, looking in particular at one Johns-Manville plant in Ontario. Finally, using the asbestos data as a case study, it looks at the incentive effects that might be generated if a system of experience rating were adopted for industrial diseases of long latency. It is hoped that the tragedy of the asbestos experience may teach us about the operation of workers' compensation systems with respect to industrial diseases of long latency and show us how our compensation systems might be improved in the future.

Determining the Extent of Impairment

The Ontario Workers' Compensation Act prescribes eligibility for a permanent disability pension as follows: "Where permanent disability results from the injury, the impairment of earning capacity of the employee shall be estimated from the nature and degree of the injury."[1] This language appears to make disability and impairment synonymous and to make both of them matters for medical determination. (For a discussion of the measurement of disability in Ontario, see Burton 1986.) The practice of the Advisory Committee on Occupational Chest Diseases (ACOCD) of the Ontario Workers' Compensation Board has been consistent with this interpretation. For example, lung function tests reveal medical impairment but not necessarily the degree to which this impairment interferes with the individual's work performance. The ACOCD will assign the individual a disability rating based on the medical impairment, whether or not this impairment interferes with the individual's current job performance.[2]

---

1. Ontario Workers' Compensation Act R.S.O., ch. 539 (1980).
2. RCA Transcript, Evidence of Dr. Jerome J.V. Vingilis (June 8, 1982), 39:49.

The Ontario Royal Commission on Asbestos found two problems with the method of rating impairment used by the ACOCD. First, the refinement of the percentages of impairment appears to exceed the precision of measurement of the tests being used. Second, an important form of impairment, psychological, is not measured at all.

With regard to the first problem, the RCA examined the current process for assessing the degree of impairment of an asbestosis victim. The extent of impairment is measured by assigned percentages, and it has been the practice of the ACOCD to use as many as ten divisions for the degree of impairment, from 10 percent to 100 percent. The ACOCD begins with a set of definitions of impairment using classes 1/2, 1, 2, 3, and 4, which are similar to classes defined by the American Medical Association (AMA) (see table 3.1). These classes are further subdivided to arrive at the full range of percentage ratings. This fine detail is provided although measurement of each of the factors that influences the rating is fraught with uncertainty and with the need for difficult judgments on which experts may differ widely. Distortions may be introduced by differences in standards applied by different X-ray readers or examining physicians, or even by the effort applied by the worker undergoing the tests (RCA 1984, 739).

The RCA concluded that this refinement in the percentages of impairment was not warranted. It chose to reduce the number of impairment classes to three (actually four, including no impairment) because it thought that greater precision was misleading. Furthermore, with only four classes, few cases would seem to be on the margin of a higher impairment rate, while with ten classes, most would be near a margin.

Using only four classes of impairment causes large differences in compensation at discrete points in the impairment continuum, however. Some analysts believe that using a small number of classes of impairment will increase disputes over impairment ratings because a change in the classification will significantly affect the amount of the disability payment. In short, with only a few broad classes, the value of winning a dispute over the classification is much greater. Whether this effect overpowers the RCA's expectation of a reduction in the number of apparently marginal cases remains to be seen.

Turning to the question of psychological impairment, we note first the AMA's definition of impairment as "any anatomic or func-

TABLE 3.1. Classes of Respiratory Impairment

	Class 1 0% Impairment	Class 2 10%–20% Impairment	Class 3 25%–35% Impairment	Class 4 50%–70% Impairment
Roentgenogram appearance	Usually normal but there may be evidence of healed or inactive chest disease including, for example, minimal nodular silicosis or pleural scars.	May be normal or abnormal.	May be normal but usually is not.	Usually is abnormal.
Dyspnea	When it occurs, it is consistent with the circumstances of activity.	Does not occur at rest and seldom during usual activities of daily living. The patient can keep pace with persons of same age and body build on the level without breathlessness but not on hills or stairs.	Does not occur at rest but does occur during the usual activities of daily living. The patient can walk a mile without dyspnea, however, but cannot keep pace on the level with others of the same age and body build.	Occurs during such activities as climbing one flight of stairs or walking 100 yards on the level, on less exertion, or even at rest.
Tests of ventilatory functions (at least two should be performed) FEV FVC$^{1.0}$ MVV	Not less than 85% of predicted.	70%–85% of predicted.	55%–70% of predicted.	Less than 55% of predicted.
Arterial oxygen saturation	Not applicable.	Not applicable.	Usually 88% or greater at rest and after exercise.	Usually less than 88% at rest and after exercise.

SOURCE: AMA, Committee on Rating of Mental and Physical Impairment, *Guides to the Evaluation of Permanent Impairment* (1971), table 8, p. 75. The RCA based its deliberations on this table; in 1984, the AMA issued a second edition containing substantial revisions.

tional abnormality or loss after maximal medical rehabilitation has been achieved" (AMA 1971).[3] Because asbestosis is irreversible, the idea of maximal medical rehabilitation is irrelevant. With respect to asbestosis, impairment thus means any anatomic or functional abnormality or loss.

As the RCA pointed out, however, medicine embraces psychological as well as physical impairment (1984, 742). The individual who is told that he or she has asbestosis learns that he or she suffers from an irreversible and normally progressive disease. Studies have shown that adverse psychological effects are associated with medical conditions that have not even produced clinical symptoms, let alone permitted the diagnosis of irreversible disease. Thus one study has found that individuals who are mislabeled as having high blood pressure show a significant decrease in their perception of well-being (Haynes et al. 1976). Another study found that when workers who were unaware that they had high blood pressure were told of their condition there was a rise in absenteeism among them, in comparison to workers who were unaware of their blood pressure. This higher rate of absenteeism has persisted over a number of years, and the most recent analysis indicates that these workers are earning about $1,000 less per person per year than their matched cohorts (Sackett et al. 1975). Because high blood pressure can be treated and does not shorten life expectancy if properly treated, the degree of attitudinal change in these otherwise healthy workers is of some significance. More serious life events can reasonably be expected to coincide with more pronounced degrees of attitudinal change. Studies have documented depression and suicide among victims of pulmonary and cardiorespiratory diseases. (See, for example, Smith 1977, Sakinofsky 1980, and Farberow et al. 1966.) One study of mortality patterns among factory workers exposed to asbestos, an excess number of whom died from respiratory disease, found thirty suicides where only seventeen might have been expected (Robinson, Lemen, and Wagoner 1979, 134).

The Ontario Workers' Compensation Board has in the past recognized the adverse psychological effects of industrial accidents.

---

3. This discussion will rely on the same 1971 AMA guide used by the RCA; a second edition, published in 1984, is now available and might lead to somewhat different results in detail, but the principles argued here remain the same.

The board has issued a guideline that states: "An employee is entitled to benefits when personal injury is sustained through an accident which arises out of and occurs in the course of employment. 'Injury' includes both physical and emotional disability."[4] It has been common practice for courts in personal injury litigation to award compensation for psychological impairment when it results from the wrong done by the defendant.

There are strong reasons to include psychological impairment in the measurement of impairment for asbestosis or other irreversible and normally progressive diseases. In the case of accidents, the victim suffers maximum loss at the time of the accident. In the case of irreversible and progressive diseases, the time of diagnosis is just the beginning. The victim knows that the worst is yet to come.

Having concluded that impairment should include psychological impairment in the case of irreversible and normally progressive diseases, the RCA went on to consider how the degree of impairment should be measured. In that the psychological impairment is in addition to the physical impairment, the degree of impairment should include the physical impairment plus an allowance for psychological impairment. If one retained the large number of classes of impairment already in use in Ontario, one could add a "psychological impairment bonus" to the impairment rating, thus increasing the compensation of a worker with a given degree of physical impairment. Instead, in that the RCA had concluded that the number of classes of impairment should be reduced to three, the following system was proposed. The board should define three classes of impairment, to be called "mild," "moderate," and "severe." These should correspond to classes 2, 3, and 4 of the AMA guides (see table 3.1) and would be defined in terms of physical impairment alone. For compensation purposes, however, psychological impairment must be included and a percentage of impairment assigned. The AMA assigns the following percentage of impairment to these three classes: class 2, 10 to 20 percent; class 3, 25 to 35 percent; and class 4, 50 to 70 percent. The RCA recommended increasing the percentages for each class, so that the classes would be assigned the following degrees of impairment: mild, 30 percent; moderate, 60 percent; severe, 100 percent (RCA 1984, 750).

---

4. "The Adjudication of Claims for Psychotraumatic Disability," Minute 11, Feb. 9, 1982, p. 4951.

The RCA recognized that an asbestosis policy that incorporates an automatic allowance for psychological impairment has implications for other compensable diseases. Unless these implications were narrowly confined, the policy might become unacceptable. The RCA suggested two boundaries to limit the application of this recognition of psychological impairment. First, it should apply only to diseases that are workplace-specific, that is, to diseases of which an industrial process is a necessary and sufficient cause. In Ontario, these would be diseases listed in schedule 3 of the Workers' Compensation Act. Asbestosis would be included, for example, while lung cancer would not. Second, the policy should apply only to chronic, irreversible diseases that shorten life expectancy. Cancers, which certainly shorten life expectancy and in some cases are workplace-specific, would not qualify because they are generally acute and not chronic disorders.

Financing Claims for Asbestos-Related Diseases

Compensation and Assessment System

Compensation in Ontario and six states. In Ontario, workers' compensation is provided by the Workers' Compensation Board. In the United States, employers may choose among three insurance systems to compensate their workers: the majority of compensation (60 percent) is provided by state or federal insurance funds, but about 20 percent of payments are from private insurance companies and an equal amount from self-insurance by employers (Price 1986). Compensation is generally available for temporary partial and total disability, for permanent partial and total disability, and for death. Asbestos diseases lead principally to permanent disability and death claims. In Ontario, temporary benefits are occasionally provided, pending a full assessment of the case.

Permanent total disability benefits are calculated as a stipulated percentage of specified base wage. Partial disability benefits are calculated as a proportion of total disability benefits according to the extent of the injury. Benefits may be adjusted if the degree of impairment changes over time. Death benefits provide a burial allowance, a possible lump-sum payment to the surviving spouse, and periodic benefits for the surviving spouse and dependents for a specified length of time. All benefits are bounded by annually adjusted

TABLE 3.2. Summary of Workers' Compensation Formulas (1983 dollars, Canadian or U.S. as relevant)

		Ontario	New York	Texas	California	Illinois	Minnesota	Michigan
Total permanent	% of base	up to 75	66⅔	66⅔	66⅔	66⅔	66⅔	80
	Base	Previous year*	8 weeks prior to injury*	Previous year*	Previous year*	Previous year*	Time of injury*	After-tax wage: highest 39 of past 52 weeks
	Weekly max.	320.19	215.00	182.00	196.00	446.40	290.00	330.00
	Weekly min.	156.00	30.00	32.00†	84.00	167.00	145.00‡	91.39§
Partial permanent		As above × % impairment	As above × % impairment	66⅔% (prior wages current capacity)	66⅔% weekly wage loss-U/C benefit	65% wage loss & dependent increment	As above × % impairment	80% after tax difference
Burial		1200	1500	1250	1500	1750	1000	1500

Death benefits	1200 to widow + 492 monthly + 136/child	Same as total permanent disability	Same as total permanent disability	Same as total permanent disability	Same as total permanent disability	50% of base—spouse only; 60% of base—one child; 66⅔% of base—more than one child	Same as total permanent disability but minimum is 182.78
Funding	State (some experience rating)	State experience rated or authorized private or self-insured	Private or self	Private or self	Private or self and state second accident fund (experience rated)	Private or self	Private or self

SOURCE: U.S. Chamber of Commerce, *Analysis of Workers' Compensation Laws, 1983.*
*Average gross weekly wage over specified time period.
†401 week, $72,982 limit.
‡Social Security deducted after $25,000 benefits paid.
δDisability pension, Social Security, retirement pension deducted.

minimums and maximums. Details of the workers' compensation systems for Ontario and for six states are provided in table 3.2.

The rules shown in table 3.2 may be used to calculate the amount that would be paid to a typical claimant in the seven jurisdictions. These total payments are shown in table 3.3. The compensation level for each type of claim is calculated on the basis of a weekly wage of $407.38 Canadian, the average weekly wage for hourly manufacturing employees in Ontario in January 1983 (Statistics Canada). For wage-based benefits, the annual benefit level used is equal to fifty-two times the lesser of the relevant proportion of this wage and the maximum value of periodic benefits in the jurisdiction.[5] For Michigan, which uses after-tax wages as a base for benefits, I assume a tax rate of 8 percent.[6] Two of these jurisdictions (California and Illinois) limit the amount that may be paid for death benefits. Converted into time limits, these limitations indicate that survivors' benefits cease after six years in California and after twenty years in Illinois.

Although there are many similarities between the Ontario and the United States workers' compensation systems, there are important differences that probably reduce the average compensation received by workers in the United States suffering from asbestos disease. Ontario has been a leader in compensating cancer of the lungs, larynx, and gastrointestinal system among asbestos-exposed workers (RCA 1984, 699–719), whereas some states still do not compensate victims of lung cancer or mesothelioma. Some states will reject claims that are not filed within a few years of last exposure, although often the disease may not manifest itself until decades later. In the United States, employers regularly challenge claims, requiring the claimant to hire a lawyer and expend considerable time and money in securing compensation or to settle for some fraction of the statutory amount. In Ontario, employers rarely challenge claims, so most claims are paid in full after routine processing and investigation. Finally, Ontario has an active outreach program to find eligible claimants (RCA 1984, 790–92). In the United States, such outreach is rare. Peter Barth (1981,

---

5. A United States-Canada conversion factor of 1.234 was used; average from International Monetary Fund. International Financial Statistics, May 1984 (1983 quarterly averages).

6. Canadian wage = $407.38 weekly × 50 = $20,369 annually, divided by exchange rate of 1.234 = $16,506 U.S. annually. Using a U.S. tax table for 1983, this salary, with standard deductions, yielded a tax rate of 8 percent.

TABLE 3.3. Undiscounted Sums of All Payments for Typical Workers' Compensation Awards (in thousands of 1983 Canadian dollars)

Jurisdiction	Death Benefits	Total Disability Plus Death*
Ontario	134	293
New York	280	418
Texas	256	372
California	62	188
Illinois	228	369
Minnesota	236	377
Michigan	341	497

*Assuming ten years of disability at 100%, followed by death.

374) found that only 29 percent of long-term asbestos workers whose illness was determined to have been caused by asbestos had even filed disability claims before death. On the one hand, in view of all these differences, it seems likely that the data for the six states listed in table 3.3 overstate the amount that an average claimant would actually receive from the United States workers' compensation systems. On the other hand, the death benefits in Ontario are considerably less than in the United States.

Assessment of employers in Ontario. The RCA (1984, 803) describes the Ontario system in some detail. The Ontario workers' compensation system collects revenue from Ontario employers by levying an assessment on the payroll of each employer. The 150,000 or more employers under schedule 1 of the Workers' Compensation Act are classified into 108 industry rate groups. A rate group may have between one and twenty-four thousand members. All employers in a given industry rate group pay the same assessment rate, based on their assessable payroll. The average assessment is under 2 percent of payroll but ranges from a low of 0.2 percent for the accounting rate group to more than 16 percent for loading and unloading cars (Weiler 1980, 81). The rate for a given group is changed annually to reflect the percentage change in the claims experience of the group from one year to the next. A single firm with several operations may have its operations classified in different rate groups. Thus, at the beginning of 1980, Johns-Manville Canada appeared in five separate

rate groups. The asbestos-cement pipe plant in Scarborough was in rate group 137: "Bricks, Blocks and Tile." The insulation plant, also in Scarborough, was in another rate group.

Within a rate group, firms may be "experience rated" if a majority of the members of the group vote in favor of experience rating. If a group is experience rated, then each firm's three-year average accident cost rate per $100 of payroll will be compared to that of the entire rate group. If the firm's cost rate is lower than that for the group, the firm may receive a credit of 25 or 50 percent of the difference between its cost rate and the group's cost rate, multiplied by the assessable payroll for the last year. If the firm's cost rate is greater than that of the rate group, a surcharge of 25 or 50 percent of the difference will be made. The rate group can choose whether it wishes to be 25 or 50 percent experience rated. There are other limits on the extent to which a firm's rating can be modified by the experience-rating plan. Importantly, the experience-rating credit or surcharge is always a fraction of the firm's assessable payroll.[7]

When an award is first made, the charges are reflected on the firm's and the rate group's accident cost statements. If the rate group is experience rated, then these costs directly affect the experience-rating charges or credits for each firm in the rate group. The medical aid and temporary compensation payments made on each claim are charged only as they are incurred, so there is no difference between what appears on the accident cost statement and what was actually paid out. With regard to pension awards for death or disability, however, the accident cost statement reflects the present value of all the expected future payments. In setting the assessment rate for the rate group, both the trend in award experience and the actual payment history are used.[8]

In addition to levying the standard assessment for a rate group on a firm and to levying experience-rating charges where appropriate, the Ontario Workers' Compensation Board can collect additional revenue from an employer with an unusually high claims rate. Section 91(7) of the Workers' Compensation Act provides that

---

7. Howard M. Iseman, Memorandum and Attachments of June 21, 1982, to Alex Joma, sent to RCA, June 22, 1982.

8. Ibid.

where the work injury frequency and the accident cost of the employer are consistently higher than that of the average in the industry in which he is engaged, the Board, as provided by the regulations, may increase the assessment for that employer by such a percentage thereof as the Board considers just, and may assess the levy the same upon the employer.

Levies made under this section are referred to as "penalty assessments" and are governed by section 6 of regulation 951 made under the act, which reads as follows:

6. (1) The increase of assessment that the Board may levy under subsection 91(7) of the Act shall be levied where an employer within an individual rating classification

(a) has incurred in two of the last three complete years of operation a deficit accident cost experience, including his proper share of administration, safety and other expenses;

(b) has incurred a lifetime deficit accident cost experience, including his proper share of administration, safety and other expenses; and

(c) has incurred during two of the last three complete years of operation a frequency rate of compensable accidents at least 25 percent higher than the average rate in the industry in which he is classified.

(2) The actual payroll for the last complete year of operation under review shall be the basis for any additional assessment to be levied under subsection (1).

(3) The first increase in assessment under subsection (1) shall be 100 percent of the assessment based on the individual rating classification of the employer.

(4) The amount of increase on any subsequent increase in assessment under subsection (1) shall be in the discretion of the Board.[9]

When the three conditions of section 6(1) in regulation 951 have been met, the board may levy a penalty assessment, which in the first year must be equal to the regular assessment for the last complete year and in subsequent years may be any amount determined by the board.

---

9. R.R.O., Reg. 951 (1980), under the Workers' Compensation Act.

The Johns-Manville Plant in Scarborough

In 1948, Johns-Manville Canada opened a manufacturing plant in Scarborough, Ontario, a suburb of Toronto. One area of the plant manufactured asbestos-cement pipe, called transite pipe, using a mixture containing four parts chrysotile and one part crocidolite asbestos. In another part of the plant, rock wool insulation was manufactured, using no asbestos. In 1955, a flex board shop was opened, and until 1970 asbestos-cement board was produced there, using only chrysotile asbestos. In 1960, the manufacture of an insulating material called thermobestos began, using amosite asbestos. The transite pipe plant closed in 1980, and the manufacture of asbestos insulation material was discontinued in the same year.

The transite pipe plant had a ventilation system to control worker exposure to dust, but dust levels have been estimated to have ranged as high as forty fibers per cubic centimeter (f/cc). Dust levels fell in the mid-1950s and then again in the early 1960s, as a new dust-collection system was installed in 1962. A more expensive investment in dust control in 1968 launched a steady reduction in dust levels that continued throughout the 1970s, until the plant was closed in 1980 (RCA 1984, 119). By 1962, average dust levels in the plant had been reduced to one-half their original levels, and by 1979 they may have been down to about 5 percent of the original levels (Dewees 1986). Testimony about working conditions in the plant revealed that some workers were literally covered in dust during the early years of the plant's operation.

This small plant, which never employed more than 714 workers, has been the source of 68 awards by the Ontario Workers' Compensation Board for asbestos-related fatalities and of 113 awards for asbestosis (RCA 1984, 117–18). Table 3.4 shows the financial impact of this record on the workers' compensation system. The first column shows the accident costs, including asbestos-related claims, attributed to this plant by the Workers' Compensation Board. By 1974, more than $500,000 in claims were being awarded every year, as asbestosis, lung cancer, and mesothelioma took their toll. During the years 1971 to 1981, a total of $6.087 million in accident costs was recorded.

The contributions by Johns-Manville to the accident fund for the same period are shown in the second column of table 3.4. These

TABLE 3.4. Costs and Receipts Summary for Johns-Manville Scarborough Pipe Plant, Rate Group 137 (all figures in thousands of dollars)

Year	Firm				Rate Group		
	Accident Costs	Receipts	Costs-Receipts Ratio	Experience-Rating Charges	Assessment Rate $/$100 payroll	Receipts*	Costs-Receipts Ratio
1971	122	62	1.98	5.8	2.25	1545	0.917
1972	88	112	0.78	8.8	2.75	2118	0.712
1973	307	141	2.17	26	2.75	2392	0.860
1974	529	170	3.11	59	3.60	3665	0.713
1975	894	253	3.53	130	3.60	3860	0.904
1976	752	444	1.69	158	4.40	5289	0.656
1977	871	369	2.36	150	5.00	6021	0.601
1978	658	333	1.98	135	5.10	6097	0.532
1979	475	355	1.34	148	4.70	5958	0.590
1980†	561	61	9.2	—	4.00	4778	0.928
1981†	831	0	—	0	3.75	4791	1.006
TOTAL	6087	2300	2.65	820	41.90	46,514	0.735

SOURCE: Howard M. Iseman, Memorandum and Attachments of June 21, 1982, to Alex Joma, sent to Royal Commission on Asbestos, June 22, 1982.

*Receipts do *not* include the experience-rating charges in 1977 and later years.

†Firm was active to May 31, 1980.

receipts include experience-rating charges for all years. The cost-receipts ratio shows that by 1973, and in every succeeding year, the contributions by Johns-Manville fell far short of covering the cost of the claims by its workers. The Workers' Compensation Board estimated that if the company had been 100 percent experience rated, it would have paid $8.285 million in assessments to the board during this period.[10] There is thus a deficit of about $6 million from this plant alone, which is borne by other employers in the province. The Ontario Royal Commission concluded, "In short, Johns-Manville has borne virtually none of the costs of the disease it has occasioned in Ontario, while it was facing a staggering cost for its involvement in similar diseases in the United States" (RCA 1984, 806). Between 1971 and 1979, when this plant was in full operation, the Johns-Manville contributions to the accident fund averaged less than 5 percent of the contributions of all firms in this rate group. The Johns-Manville claims, however, represented more than 15 percent of the claims of the group.

Tragically, the asbestos-related awards made through 1981 probably represent less than half the morbidity and mortality that will ultimately result from the operation of that plant. Julian Peto, Brian Henderson, and Malcolm Pike (1981) estimated that the exposure of workers to asbestos in the United States before 1965 would cause 150,000 cancer deaths, only one-quarter of which had occurred by 1980. Many of the anticipated deaths would occur in the first quarter of the next century. I have elsewhere attempted to predict the future claims that may arise from past exposure at the Scarborough Johns-Manville plant (Dewees 1986). I assumed that the stock of claims that existed from 1978 to 1982 would remain at the same level until the year 2010, at which time the least severe partial disability claims would cease. I assumed the last fatality claim would occur in the year 2025. The projections this method provides of future disease accord with those presented in various epidemiological studies that show disease peaking in the mid-1990s and declining thereafter (MacAvoy 1982, 13–16; RCA 1984, 787–88; Selikoff 1981, 133).

The disease resulting from the operation of the Johns-Manville plant will continue to emerge for the next forty years or so, leading

---

10. RCA Exhibit IV-5, Workers' Compensation Board, Inter-Divisional Communication, from John C. Neal to Alan G. MacDonald.

to claims that may cost considerably more than those that have already been approved. The contributions by Johns-Manville, however, ceased in 1980, even though the company continues to do business in Ontario and has not filed for bankruptcy in Canada. The financing system for workers' compensation in Ontario is based on multiplying the assessable payroll of the firm by a number representing the assessment rate for the group and any increment representing experience rating. If the assessable payroll drops to zero, then the firm's contribution to the Workers' Compensation Board's accident fund also drops to zero. In that a firm may have its operations classified in more than one rate group, it is possible for a firm to continue to do business in Ontario yet cease to contribute to the fund on behalf of one of its operations. Thus the moment that Johns-Manville Canada ceased operation at its pipe plant in Scarborough, the payroll terminated, and Johns-Manville's contribution to the accident fund on behalf of its employees of that plant also dropped to zero. In 1981, claims, including disease claims attributed to the Scarborough pipe plant, totaled $831,000. Receipts from Johns-Manville for that pipe plant were zero, as were experience-rating charges. On the same property, Johns-Manville continues to do business in its insulation operations, and its other businesses in the province also continue to operate. Claims that are paid after an employer has left a rate group are borne by the remaining members of that group, unless the board determines that this imposes an unreasonable burden on these employers, in which case they will be borne by the accident fund generally.

As noted above, the Workers' Compensation Board has the authority to levy a penalty assessment on an employer with an unusually high claims rate. Although the Johns-Manville pipe plant left a deficit from 1971 to 1981 of close to $6 million in the accident fund, no penalty assessment has ever been levied against the company. Because Johns-Manville's accident frequency was below the average of its rate group, no penalty assessment could have been made until 1980, by which time the frequency of compensable accidents was 25 percent higher than the average for the rate group for two of the last three years. The Ontario Workers' Compensation Board did not levy a penalty assessment, apparently because it is board policy not to levy such an assessment on a plant after it has closed.[11] The RCA concluded

---

11. Ibid.

that the statute would allow the board to levy a penalty assessment
on a closed plant in any year in which the plant had a payroll, and
Johns-Manville did have some payroll in 1980 (RCA 1984, 808). The
RCA recommended that the board levy a penalty assessment against
this Johns-Manville plant, in the maximum amount allowed by the
statute and regulations, which would be $60,000. Although this
amount is small compared to the company's deficit in the accident
fund, the assessment would signal the board's concern about the
deficit.

Finally, because the RCA was not empowered to determine
past wrongdoing, it did not pass judgment on any knowledge that
Johns-Manville might have had in 1948 about the health hazards to
which its workers might be exposed. The RCA was cognizant, however, of the possibility that a firm might at some time knowingly expose workers to health hazards without informing the workers of
the hazard they faced. To discourage such behavior, the RCA recommended that the board be given a right to sue an employer whose
disease claims exceeded his or her contributions to the accident
fund when the board had reason to believe that the employer
withheld from employees knowledge he or she possessed about the
hazardous nature of a substance to which workers were exposed.
The amount to be recovered in this lawsuit would be twice the
value of the employer's disease claims caused by the substance
in question. If such a lawsuit were successful, half the proceeds
would be retained by the Workers' Compensation Board and the
other half would be distributed to the claimants involved (RCA
1984, 809).

On what basis might we assess the performance of the Ontario
workers' compensation system in dealing with the disease experience
of the Johns-Manville plant? The Workers' Compensation Board's
performance in compensating workers appears commendable, especially compared to the experience in the United States. Although the
RCA recommended extensive changes in the board's procedures for
dealing with claims, it concluded that the board is, "in the sphere of
asbestos disease, one of the most progressive compensation agencies
in the world" (RCA 1984, 17). In terms of fairness among employers,
the RCA was clearly disturbed that this firm had borne so small a
portion of the cost of the disease that had occurred at its plant. While
there may be debate over whether today's shareholders and managers
should bear the full burden of the cost of disease resulting from

decisions made more than thirty years ago, by other managers, few have argued that they should bear as small a share as they have in Ontario.

Finally, we can assess the incentives that the Johns-Manville experience creates for firms that may in the future be in the position of creating a situation in which there is a possibility of significant health risks that are not precluded by prevailing workplace safety regulations. Economists argue in general that efficiency is improved if externalities are internalized, that is, if actors face the full costs of the results of their decisions. While this prescription is often extended to the arena of occupational health and safety, other economists with expertise in this field are often skeptical about the practical benefits that might arise from creating these incentives. Peter Barth (1983, 4) has argued, for example, that experience rating should be eliminated for diseases of long latency. He argues that there are no benefits from experience rating with respect to such diseases because the current management is not responsible for them and cannot take steps to prevent future claims whose seeds were sown in the past. Furthermore, there are costs to experience rating. The employer may be induced to conceal hazardous exposures from workers and to disrupt claims, which, because of the long delay, are often difficult to support even in the most meritorious cases. Paul M. Weiler, a long-time analyst of the Ontario workers' compensation system, concluded that the long delay between the exposure of the worker and the payment of a disease or death claim would render experience rating ineffective increasing a significant incentive to reduce workplace health risks (1983, 130).

I will not here resolve this debate over experience rating. The Johns-Manville experience may, however, be used as a data base for evaluating the incentive that might be created if a vigorous experience-rating system or a liability system such as that proposed by the Ontario Royal Commission were adopted for industrial diseases of long latency.

Deterrent Effect of Imposing Disease Costs on the Firm

Model of the Firm

To evaluate the economic incentives created by imposing on a firm the total cost of all the disease claims that were allowed by a workers' compensation agency, it is necessary to have a model of the firm and how it evaluates the costs that it faces. This model must incorporate time and discounting, because of the long delay for asbestos-related diseases and other diseases of long latency between any decision on worker exposure and the occurrence of workers' compensation claims. The model presented here may be used to evaluate the financial liability that may arise in the future as a result of exposure to a hazardous substance today.

The model depends upon assumptions about information the firm and workers have regarding the health hazards presented by the substance. If workers know the risks and the dose-response relationship, then they should bargain for a compensating wage differential that will in turn create an incentive for the firm to reduce worker exposure. Any workers' compensation benefits will tend to reduce the compensating wage demanded, but to the extent that the premiums are risk rated, the incentive on the employer to reduce exposure will be retained. If workers are ignorant of the risks, as they were about asbestos in the 1950s and may be about new chemical risks in the future, then they will not demand a compensating wage differential. If the firm knows or can discover the risks and the dose-response relationship, its incentive to reduce worker exposure must arise, absent government regulation, from the prospect of future liability for disease arising from current exposure.

I assume that the objective of the firm is to maximize its value. This requires that the firm maximize the present discounted value of its expected after-tax cash flow. This objective is shown in equation 3.1

$$\text{Max } V_o = \sum_{t=0}^{\infty} \frac{E\{CF_t\}}{(1+r_w)^t} \tag{3.1}$$

where E = expected value; CF_t = after-tax cash flow in year t; r_w = weighted after-tax cost of capital = $\alpha r_e + (1-\tau)(1-\alpha)r_b$; α = fraction of capital in equity; r_e = cost of equity; τ = marginal corporate income tax rate; r_b = cost of debt.

In equation 3.1, the firm discounts future cash flows using the weighted after-tax cost of capital as the discount rate. This cost of capital is itself the rate of return paid on equity times the fraction of the capital represented by equity plus the rate of return on bonds times the fraction of capital represented by bonds multiplied by one minus the corporate income tax rate, to indicate the after-tax cost of that deductible bond interest. I assume that demand for the product is determined exogenously and is unrelated to occupational health protection. The cost of protecting occupational health is separable from the remainder of the production function. Workers are ignorant of the risks, so there is no compensating wage differential.

The cash flow in equation 3.1 consists of revenues less expenses less taxes less capital investment. The taxes in turn are calculated as revenues minus expenses minus depreciation. Because I am only interested in evaluating the impact of future expenses in the form of workers' compensation liability, revenues may be held constant and capital investment and depreciation may be ignored. Cash flow may therefore be defined as the after-tax flow of liability costs, or

$$CF_t = (-C_t)(1-\tau)$$

where C_t represents liability costs in year t.

The financial model requires some market data and some firm-specific data. For market data, I rely primarily on Roger Ibbotson and Rex Sinquefield (1979, 12). They report the average rate of return on corporate debt, from 1926 to 1977, as 1.5 percent in real terms. I will use 1.5 percent for r_b. For the risk-free rate of return, r_f, I use the real return on short-term treasury bills, reported as 0.0 percent. For the market rate of return, r_m, I use the average annual real rate of return on common stock, or 6.4 percent.

During the 1950s and 1960s, Johns-Manville was financed almost exclusively by equity. I will represent Johns-Manville's capital structure with $\alpha = 0.98$. I have elsewhere calculated the cost of equity capital for Johns-Manville and found it to be 7.27 percent, yielding a weighted cost of capital for the firm of 7.127 percent (Dewees 1986, table 2).

Why use this complicated model rather than simply discounting the future costs at a reasonable rate? First, corporate taxes are an important fact of life, and corporations devote considerable time and talent to determining their tax liability and arranging their business affairs to allow for the tax consequences of their actions. To ignore corporate income taxes is to ignore a major factor in corporate decision making. Second, the real complexity in the model is in the calculation of the corporate discount rate. Yet there has been great debate about the "proper" discount rate to use in evaluating corporate decisions, and the model proposed here is regarded by experts in economics and finance as the most appropriate (Brealey and Myers 1981, pt. 3).

Still, even if this model is theoretically superior to a simple discounting of cash flows, it would hardly be worth the trouble it involves if it gave the same answer as a simpler model. By inspection, however, one can see that the model makes a great deal of difference indeed. With a corporate income tax rate of 0.5, the after-tax impact of any liability is half what it would be if taxes were ignored. Furthermore, the discount rate is significantly higher for Johns-Manville than for an average firm (Dewees 1986, table 2). The presence of the corporate income tax reduces the present value of future liabilities, and the higher discount rate lowers them still further. It would be a serious error to ignore factors that will cut the final results to less than half those of a naive calculation. This model recognizes that the ultimate effect of the corporate income tax is to subsidize all business expenses, including liability for workers' compensation assessments or tort awards.

Value of Workers' Compensation Claims from the Scarborough Plant

Table 3.4 presents the total amounts paid in compensation to Johns-Manville workers, including compensation for accidents as well as for asbestos-related diseases. To evaluate the present value in 1948, when the plant was first opened, of the liability for asbestos-related workers' compensation claims, a record of the individual claims is combined with the 1983 compensation formula to determine the workers' compensation costs that would be charged to the company. I also rely on a model of future disease to determine the future claims that might arise. (See Dewees 1986 for more details.) The calculations are repeated using the compensation formulas of six states, for comparison.

Applying Ontario benefits to Ontario claims data is straightforward. Applying benefits from other workers' compensation systems to Ontario claims data poses several problems. Most American work-

TABLE 3.5. Present Value of Net Cash Flow Based on Workers'
Compensation Claims Costs (in millions of 1983 Canadian dollars)

Jurisdiction	All Diseases
Ontario	−0.94
New York	−1.44
Texas	−1.26
California	−0.79
Illinois	−1.36
Minnesota	−1.23
Michigan	−1.62
$r_w = 7.127$	

SOURCE: Dewees 1986. Based on 1983 compensation formulas. See table 3.2.

ers' compensation systems operate quite differently from the Ontario
system. Claims are regularly challenged by employers. Available de-
fenses include delay in filing the claim and nonrecognition of the
disease, as well as arguments that the employee contracted the disease
when working for a second asbestos user or manufacturer. Claims
may take a long time to be resolved, and legal fees, while fixed by
statute, may still amount to 20 percent of a successful claim (Selikoff
1981, 494). Often claims are settled out of court for a fraction of the
statutory benefits.[12] In court, the judge may award lower benefits than
applicable for the type of disability, for reasons related to the proof
of the particular employers' responsibility and not to the severity of
the condition (489–90). Actual payouts by employers may be higher
or lower than in Ontario, depending on many factors. Our estimates
of worker benefits for claims brought in Ontario considerably overstate what we believe would be the experience of these workers under
United States compensation laws.

Table 3.5 shows this present value using the workers' compensation awards in seven jurisdictions to calculate the amount of the
future liability. This is, in effect, a calculation of the firm's liability in
the face of 100 percent experience rating of its workers' compensation
assessment. The net present value in 1948 of the liability ranges from

12. In New Jersey, the employer offers a settlement in noncontested claims,
which the worker may accept or reject. If it is rejected, the case will go to trial. Overall
in the United States, one-third of asbestos claims are settled. In New Jersey, the median
claim took nineteen months between filing and resolution. Settled claims, in the cohort
of New Jersey workers examined in Selikoff's study, never exceeded a lump-sum benefit
of $30,000 (1981, 7, 8, 483, 515).

-0.79 million in California to -1.62 million in Michigan. This value is less than the annual claims cost in Ontario in the late 1970s and less than the capital cost of the controls installed in 1962. While this liability is not trivial, neither is it large.

I conclude that the long delays between worker exposure and the awarding of worker compensation, combined with a private corporate discount rate of more than 7 percent, greatly reduce the present value of future workers' compensation liability, even with 100 percent risk rating. The incentive effects of such risk rating seem modest indeed.

Deterrence for Regulated Substances

We have just analyzed what has been termed an occupational health disaster, in which a high proportion of workers have contracted or will contract debilitating and often fatal diseases. At the time the workers were exposed, there was no regulation of the substance and apparently little concern about that exposure on the part of the employer, the workers, or the government. The exposures were, by all accounts, considerable—greatly above the exposures found in manufacturing operations today. Still, the present value of the workers' compensation liability is not large. Is there any role for experience rating in connection with diseases that arise from exposure to regulated substances? Once regulatory authorities have tackled the problem of occupational disease, with the myriad regulations that have now appeared both in Canada and in the United States, can experience rating of workers' compensation premiums provide any added incentive to reduce exposure?

The simple answer appears to be no. Many potentially harmful substances are regulated to the point where the marginal cost of further control is enormous, often tens of millions of dollars per life saved (Dewees and Daniels 1986). The remaining risks are very small compared to the risks faced by asbestos workers in the 1950s. Thus the incentive effect of experience rating on today's exposures must be even smaller than that calculated above. This financial incentive must be trivial compared to the high cost of further protection under strict regulation.

There remains, however, an exception. One cannot rule out the occurrence at some time in the future of another occupational health disaster similar to the asbestos disaster. Governments may fail to regulate a dangerous substance. Or a firm may unknowingly, or knowingly, expose its workers to high concentrations of a dangerous regulated substance in violation of the regulations. A firm may expose workers to a substance that it believes may be hazardous but that has not been declared dangerous at the time. The presence of experience rating for diseases of long latency would provide an incentive for the firm to detect such situations and to avoid excessive worker exposure.

In addition, the use of experience rating may be supported on the grounds of horizontal equity. Whatever the incentive effects, it seems unjust to hold all employers responsible for the disease costs occasioned by the actions of one employer. The Ontario RCA expressed this concern in defense of its recommendation that, especially for asbestos employers, the Workers' Compensation Board give consideration to more rather than less experience rating (RCA 1984, recommendation 14.10).

We cannot, however, overlook the substantial problems inherent in experience rating for diseases of long latency. The RCA noted that Ontario employers have rarely resisted workers' compensation claims by their employees and have sometimes assisted workers in filing these claims. Experience rating that passed large portions of the cost of such claims on to the employer would likely change employers' attitudes and perhaps lead them to contest such claims, as often occurs in the United States. Contesting claims would increase the cost of administering the system and perhaps discourage the filing of some legitimate claims.

A second problem is the difficulty encountered in attempting to extract large amounts of money from an employer for past actions. In the United States, Johns-Manville declared bankruptcy in the face of an avalanche of personal injury lawsuits related to its asbestos products, and plaintiffs are fighting over funds that appear to fall short of satisfying all claims. In Ontario, the Scarborough Johns-Manville plant closed, cutting off liability for past workers' compensation claims from that plant. Unless the stream of claims is small compared to the profits from current operations, one may expect firms to arrange their affairs to minimize these claims, whether they arise through tort litigation or through experience-rated workers' compensation assessments.

A third problem is that the horizontal equity achieved in forcing a firm to pay today for the harm arising from past exposures may be more symbolic than real. The officers and directors who sanctioned the past exposures, and the shareholders who profited from them, are generally not today's officers, directors, and shareholders. While some may celebrate the punishment of the corporation, it is not clear that those who suffer are in fact the proper objects of righteous indignation.

Conclusions

This chapter does not offer a panacea for the problem of compensating victims of industrial diseases of long latency. I have suggested that workers who contract progressive fatal diseases that shorten life expectancy and that arise exclusively from exposure to an industrial process should be compensated for psychological as well as physical impairment, to recognize the real suffering that begins when the worker learns of his or her diagnosis.

For the problem of protecting workers from diseases of long latency arising from exposure to hazardous substances, I have found no simple solution. With all its faults, the regulatory system appears to offer important protection to workers, particularly the unorganized and uninformed. Employee demands through the collective bargaining system offer additional protection. It appears that risk rating of workers' compensation premiums can play a backstop role, offering incentives in cases in which the risks are high and the regulatory and bargaining systems have failed to afford adequate protection. It must be recognized, however, that its effects are likely to be limited both in magnitude and in scope and that the other elements mentioned above are of much broader importance.

4·WORKERS' COMPENSATION, WAGES, AND THE RISK OF INJURY

Ronald G. Ehrenberg

In many respects the structures of the workers' compensation and unemployment insurance systems are similar. Each is actually a system of individual state systems. Both are financed by a payroll tax that is imperfectly experience rated. Both provide insurance against an adverse consequence (work injury or unemployment) that leads to time away from work; the incidence and duration of these events are at least partially determined by both employer *and* employee behavior. Both systems provide, at least for temporary events, a structure of benefits that ties compensation to a worker's previous earnings.

Because of these similarities, it is not inappropriate for an individual such as myself, who has conducted some research on the unemployment insurance system but none on the workers' compensation system, to provide an analysis and summary of the effects of the latter on work injury experience. Indeed, one contribution of this chapter will be to point out how lessons learned from research on other forms of social insurance can be applied to research on workers' compensation. Nonetheless, there are important differences in, and complexities of, the workers' compensation system that analyses of it must take into account; these are highlighted as well.

I begin with a brief overview of the characteristics of the workers' compensation system. I then sketch some simple labor market models that suggest how the system might affect employee compensation and the frequency and duration of work-related injuries. Critical analysis of the empirical literature on these effects follows.

Characteristics of the Workers' Compensation System

As mentioned above, the workers' compensation system is actually a composite of state systems; variations in the values of key parameters across states provide the basis of many of the empirical analyses discussed later.[1] Workers' compensation benefits are a form of no-fault insurance in which employers agree to pay specified benefits to workers injured on the job in return for limited liability. The no-fault aspect of it, however, still leaves employers the right to challenge claims on such grounds as that the injury did not take place on the job, the injury is not as severe as the employee claims, or an injured employee is not returning to work as quickly as is possible. The frequency with which claims are challenged may well vary across states (Burton and Berkowitz 1982, 80).

Five types of benefits are paid under the workers' compensation system. First, *medical benefits* are provided to injured workers. Second, *temporary total disability* benefits are paid to injured workers who temporarily cannot work at all but for whom full recovery is expected. There typically is a waiting period, which varies across states, before benefits commence, and the benefits are specified as a fraction of preinjury earnings. This fraction, the income-replacement rate, usually is set at two-thirds; however, each state specifies a minimum and maximum benefit level (the latter is often tied to average weekly earnings in the state).

Third, *permanent total disability* benefits are paid when an individual is permanently prevented from working at all. The structure of benefits is similar to temporary total disability benefits; in some cases there is also a maximum duration of time in which benefits may be received.

Fourth, *permanent partial disability* benefits are paid for injuries that are expected, even after the healing period, to result in permanent physical impairments and/or limitations on earnings capacity

---

1. Much more detailed discussions of the workers' compensation system are presented elsewhere. For example, see Burton 1983, Burton and Berkowitz 1982, Victor 1983, Victor, Cohen, and Phelps 1982, and Worrall 1983. My discussion, which is unabashedly pirated from them, is necessarily brief and nontechnical.

and/or reductions in actual earnings. In many states, these benefits are determined ex ante (before the permanent consequences of the injury are experienced) and are not conditional on ex post loss of earnings, while in a few states, benefits for certain types of injuries (nonscheduled ones) depend on actual earnings loss. In these latter states, benefits for other types of injuries (scheduled ones) do not depend on actual earnings loss. In most states, however, nonscheduled benefits do not depend on actual earnings loss. Finally, *burial and survival benefits* are paid on death claims, which are a small share of claims. Permanent partial disability and temporary total disability are, in order, the two most important categories of indemnity claims, based on dollar expenditures (together representing more than 80 percent of workers' compensation indemnity costs), while temporary total disability claims are by far the most frequent type of claims.

Most firms purchase insurance against workers' compensation claims either from a government or private insurance carrier, depending on the state (some states offer both options). Premiums are paid by employers as a percentage of total payroll. Small employers are manually rated, or charged a premium based on historical experience of the industry class to which they belong. As a result, their workers' compensation payroll tax is imperfectly experience rated in that, at the margin, they do not bear the full cost of workers' compensation benefits paid to their employees.

As an employer becomes larger, the manual rate is modified more and more to reflect the injury experience of the firm. Indeed, the rates of very large firms depend solely on their own historical experience; they are said to be perfectly experience rated (in principle, they bear the full costs of workers' compensation benefits received by their employees). Large firms also have the option of self-insuring, which also leads to perfect experience rating. In general, over a wide range of firm sizes, workers' compensation costs are imperfectly experience rated, with the extent of experience rating increasing with firm size.[2]

Two final points warrant mention here. First, workers' com-

---

2. A more detailed discussion of experience rating is found in Victor 1983. John Burton has stressed to me that even very large firms are likely to insure themselves against catastrophes and thus not to have a 100 percent perfect experience rating.

pensation benefits are not taxable; thus their net worth depends on a worker's family income bracket. Second, recipients of workers' compensation benefits may receive other forms of insurance benefits that are conditioned on either their disability status (e.g., Social Security or private disability payments) or their family income level (e.g., food stamps). Empirical analyses of the incentive effects of workers' compensation benefits should (but typically do not) take into account both the tax treatment of workers' compensation benefits and the existence of these other forms of benefits. Both omissions may distort estimates of the incentive effects of workers' compensation.

Workers' Compensation Effects: Theory

Consider a simplified world in which the labor market is competitive, workers have perfect information about the risks of injury associated with each job, and there are no barriers to mobility between jobs.[3] Suppose also that firms differ in their production technology; that each technology has certain inherent risks of injury associated with it, which can be reduced if firms expend resources to do so; and that the marginal cost (to the employer) of reducing risks varies across firms.

Assume also, initially, that workers value positively their expected earnings per period (earnings times the probability of not being injured) and value negatively the probability of being injured. Workers will move to firms whose wage rates–risk of injury combination maximizes their well-being and, if all workers have identical preferences, firms with higher risks of injury would have to pay higher wages to attract workers. The mobility of workers would thus lead to *fully compensating* wage differentials, or wage differentials that compensate workers for the disutility they would suffer from risk of injury.[4]

In such a world, firms would offer the wage rates–risk of injury combination so that their marginal cost for injury reduction would

---

3. The discussion here draws heavily on previous discussions. See the sources cited in note 1 as well as Chelius 1974, 1977, and 1983. I have again abstracted from many details of the program and ignored a host of issues.

4. If workers have different degrees of aversion to risk, they will sort themselves across firms so that those with the least aversion will be in the high-risk firms. The market wage differential between low- and high-risk firms will understate the wage differential that workers at low-risk firms would demand to move to high-risk firms.

equal their marginal benefits from injury reduction. The former includes the costs of resources devoted to preventing accidents, while the latter includes the lower bill for wages associated with the lower accident rate, less downtime in production, and reduced hiring and training costs of replacements for injured workers. If the marginal cost of preventing accidents varied across firms, different firms would offer different "wage-injury rate packages."

In such a world, the introduction of workers' compensation benefits that were perfectly experience rated (and contained no loading or administrative charges) would not affect the injury rate at any firm. Rather, because workers' compensation benefits would now compensate workers if they were injured, smaller compensating wage differentials would be required to attract workers to firms with high injury rates. Thus higher workers' compensation benefits should lead to lower wages at each firm. Workers' compensation benefits would not affect the injury rate that was optimal from each firm's perspective, since the firm's reduction in wage costs would just be offset by the new workers' compensation costs.

Suppose, instead, that workers' compensation benefits were not perfectly experience rated. In this case, the reduction in wage costs resulting from the payment of benefits would be greater than the employers' liability for the benefits. The marginal benefits of preventing accidents would therefore fall, and employers would spend fewer resources on injury reduction. In this case, imperfect experience rating would lead to a *higher* injury rate than would exist either in the absence of the workers' compensation system or in the presence of a workers' compensation system that was perfectly experience rated.

Of course all of the above presupposes a perfectly competitive labor market in which wage differentials arise to compensate workers fully for risk of injury. In such a world, if workers are risk neutral, there is in fact little rationale for a workers' compensation system.[5] If, however, fully compensating wage differentials do not arise, the

---

5. If workers were risk averse, they would prefer the certainty of workers' compensation benefits when an injury occurs to a risk premium with the same expected value. In this case, the introduction of workers' compensation benefits would improve workers' welfare. One should caution, however, that in this situation, the resulting decline in the risk premium would exceed the actuarial value of the workers' compensation benefits, which would decrease employers' incentives to prevent risks. Thus, again, the injury rate might rise relative to the injury rate that would prevail in the absence of the system.

predicted effects of workers' compensation benefits are quite different.

Consider again the case of a perfectly experience-rated workers' compensation system in which employers bear the full costs of the workers' compensation benefits paid to their employees. In this situation, in which wage differentials do not initially fully compensate workers for risk of injury, the marginal costs of injuries for employers would rise in the presence of workers' compensation benefits (wages would not fall sufficiently to offset the cost of benefits). As such, employers would have increased incentives to take actions to reduce injury rates, and one would expect to observe a decline in the injury rate.[6]

From the employers' side of the labor market, then, the effect of the workers' compensation system or higher workers' compensation benefits on resources employers devote to reducing work injuries, and hence the injury rate, is ambiguous. If wage differentials do fully compensate workers for the risk of injury and the system is imperfectly experience rated, the injury rate may actually increase. If wage differentials are not fully compensating and the system is perfectly experience rated, the injury rate will decrease. Empirical analyses are required to resolve the ambiguity.

One should distinguish, however, between incentives for employers to increase resources devoted to injury prevention, and thus decrease the injury rate, and incentives for employers to reduce both the incidence and duration of workers' compensation claims. As long as workers' compensation benefits are at least partially experience rated, higher benefits will increase employers' incentives both to challenge claims and to encourage injured workers to speed their recovery and return to work. Even if increasing benefits does not alter employer resources devoted to injury prevention, it may affect the number and duration of claims.

The above discussion focuses on the employer side of the labor market. Increasing temporary total workers' compensation benefits may also affect injury rates and claims by influencing employee behavior. First, higher benefits may reduce the disutility workers feel

---

6. In a world where all workers' compensation costs are not shifted to workers, in the form of lower wages, or to consumers, in the form of higher prices, there also would be employment effects. See Ehrenberg, Hutchens, and Smith 1978 for a discussion of the evidence on the shifting of the payroll tax.

when they have *minor* and *temporary* illnesses. Thus higher benefits may reduce the precautions they take on the job to prevent accidents that are unlikely to lead to serious permanent injuries. Second, higher benefit levels increase employees' incentives to file claims for minor injuries in which the need to remain temporarily off the job is ambiguous.[7] Third, to the extent that workers at least partially control the speed at which rehabilitation from temporary disability occurs, higher benefits increase workers' incentives to prolong their recovery period.

From workers' perspectives, then, higher temporary total disability benefit levels may lead to increased workers' compensation claims. Whether this is due to an increase in injury rates because workers use less precaution or to an increase in the probability of filing a claim, given a minor injury, is important to determine. Higher benefits may also lead to longer durations for individual claims; however, this does not imply that the average duration of claims would lengthen. If the higher benefits induce a lot of claims based on less severe injuries, the average duration of claims might actually fall.

Permanent partial disability benefits may also affect workers' compensation claim rates and the supply of labor by disabled workers to the market. One must distinguish here between scheduled and nonscheduled benefits that are not contingent on actual earnings loss and nonscheduled benefits that are. In the former case, benefits typically are not contingent on work effort after the benefit determination date; they are specified as a lump-sum or weekly amount for a fixed duration. These benefits increase the injured individual's wealth (assuming medical expenses have also been fully compensated). To the extent that individuals value leisure time as well as income, higher scheduled benefits should lead to fewer hours of work and a reduced fraction of time in the labor force.

In some states, however, such as New York and Florida, nonscheduled benefits are specified as a fraction of earnings losses (preinjury earnings minus postinjury actual earnings), subject to maximum benefit levels. Benefits here are contingent on work effort and, like any income-transfer system of this type (e.g., Aid to Families with

---

7. For both of these reasons, a decline in the length of the waiting period before benefits can be received would also increase the number of workers' compensation claims.

Dependent Children), higher wage-replacement rates encourage reduced labor force participation and hours of work. Furthermore, the formulas used to compute benefits under such systems do not take into account that economic conditions may affect the earnings prospects of injured workers; benefit levels do *not* depend on local unemployment rates. Because higher unemployment rates reduce the actual earnings prospects of some injured workers relative to their nonscheduled permanent partial benefits, one would expect permanent partial claim rates for nonscheduled benefits in these states to increase when unemployment rates are high.

In sum, workers' compensation benefit levels, operating through both the employer and the employee side of the market, should be expected to influence the magnitude of compensating wage differentials, efforts by employers to reduce injury rates, injury rates per se, the number and types of workers' compensation claims, the durations of different types of claims, and the labor force attachment and hours of work of injured workers. It is to an analysis of the empirical evidence on many of these effects that I now turn.

Compensating Wage Differentials

The first issue is whether markets "work" in the sense that wage differentials arise to compensate workers for exposure to risk of injury. Numerous studies have used cross-section data, with either establishments or individuals as the units of observation, and attempted to ascertain if wage rates are positively associated with various measures of injury risk (fatal accident rates, nonfatal accident rates, workdays lost as a result of accident rates, and so on), after other personal characteristics that should influence wages (e.g., education, experience) are controlled for.[8]

These studies uniformly tend to find that there is a positive association between fatal accident rates and wages. The relationship between nonfatal accident rates and wages is less well established, however; it appears in some studies but not in others. Most studies

---

8. The pre-1979 studies are summarized in Smith 1979. Examples of later studies include Brown 1980, Burton 1983, Butler and Worrall 1983, Dickens 1984, Freeman and Medoff 1981, Olson 1981, Ruser 1986, Smith and Dillingham 1984, Viscusi 1978, 1979, and 1980, and Viscusi and Moore 1987. Recent attempts that use longitudinal data include Duncan and Holmlund 1983 and Moore and Viscusi 1987.

indicate that the magnitude of compensating wage differentials is larger in the union sector than in the nonunion sector,[9] an expected result given that accident rates tend to be higher in the union sector and that unions may serve the role of winning wage differentials at the bargaining table to compensate their members for unfavorable job characteristics when "the market" fails to produce such differentials (see Worrall and Butler 1983 and Duncan and Stafford 1980). The result, that compensating wage differentials are larger in the union sector, is not unique to risk of injury. Others have found similar results for such unfavorable job characteristics as mandatory overtime requirements (Ehrenberg and Schumann 1984).

Somewhat surprisingly, many studies fail to consider the possibility that interstate, intertemporal, or interindustry variations in the generosity of workers' compensation systems, as measured by income-replacement rates, might affect the magnitude of the differentials in compensating wages. The few studies that have *do* find that higher workers' compensation income-replacement rates reduce the magnitude of the wage differential paid for a given risk of injury.[10] One study has also found that higher risks of injury are associated with higher levels of fringe benefits and with higher wages (Dorsey 1983).

Unfortunately, this voluminous literature provides very little that is of use for public policy. Presumably one wants to know if (1) the market is providing appropriate incentives for employers to take actions to reduce injury rates and (2) the market is *fully* compensating workers for risk of injury. As discussed below, no answer to either of these questions is provided by these studies.

With respect to the first question, the issue is really whether the positive association between wages and risk-of-injury measures reflects a compensating wage differential for risk of injury. Jobs may offer a variety of undesirable working conditions in addition to risk

---

9. See Dickens 1984, Freeman and Medoff 1981, Olson 1981, and Viscusi 1979, for example. Smith and Dillingham (1984) find this result in 1973 data but not in 1977 or 1979 data. Ruser (1986) finds the result only for females.

10. See Arnould and Nichols 1983, Butler 1983, Dorsey 1983, Dorsey and Walzer 1983, Ruser 1986, and Viscusi and Moore 1987. While all these studies agree that higher workers' compensation benefits are associated with lower wages, holding injury rates constant, they differ on how the level of workers' compensation benefits affects the *marginal* effect of injury rates on wages. For example, Ruser (1986) finds that higher benefits do not alter the wage-injury rate trade off, while Viscusi and Moore (1987) find higher benefits *increase* the marginal compensating differential for injury risk.

of injury; these may include having to work in a noisy environment, having to do repetitive tasks, being required to do heavy lifting, and lacking the opportunity to make independent judgments. Many of these job characteristics are probably highly correlated with risk of injury on the job, and workers may demand wage premiums to accept them. As a result, when one omits these other job characteristics from the analysis, any effect they have on wages is captured by the risk-of-injury variable. Thus one may well overstate the true magnitude of the compensating wage differentials for risk of injury.[11] When a few investigators have included other working conditions along with risk of injury in wage equations, the risk-of-injury variables tended not to be significantly associated with wages (see, for example, Brown 1980). Whether this is due to the high collinearity of the working conditions variables (which makes estimates imprecise) or to the nonexistence of a true wage–risk of injury differential cannot be determined. In either case, the evidence on the existence of compensating wage differentials *for* risk of injury is not as well established as the various studies would have us believe.

Suppose we ignore this problem and assume that wage differentials for risk of injury do exist. How could one hope to decide that their magnitudes are sufficiently large to permit one to conclude that they *fully* compensate workers for the disutility associated with risk of injury? Only if they are, as is implicitly assumed in a discussion of the subject in chapter 6 of the *1987 Economic Report of the President*, is the case for government intervention to improve occupational safety weakened. Only if they are can one derive "value-of-life" estimates from them to use in benefit/cost studies of occupational safety and health interventions. (See Ehrenberg and Smith 1988, 272–76, for examples of such benefit/cost analyses.)

Now, if one truly believes that all labor markets are competitive, it is a tautology that whatever wage differentials are generated by these markets will be "fully compensating" ones. Once one allows for market imperfections, however, the question becomes an empirical one. The mere existence of *some* wage differential does *not* imply that it is a fully compensating one.

Estimates of the compensating wage differentials associated

---

11. This criticism is really directed at the whole "compensating wage differential" literature and is not unique to studies of risk of injury.

with the risk of fatal injury at the workplace suggest that individuals are paid a premium of 1 to 4 percent of their wages to compensate them for existing risks of fatal injury; this leads (given the magnitude of fatal injury rates) to imputed values of lives in the range of $200,000 to $3,500,000 (see Smith 1979). Researchers have no way of evaluating (nor have they even tended to consider) whether differentials in this range truly fully compensate workers for risk of fatal injury.

As a result, the potential usefulness for public policy in occupational safety of estimates of compensating wage differentials for injury risk is limited. On the one hand, if these estimates truly reflect differentials paid for risk of injury, they may provide only lower-bound estimates of the value of life. On the other hand, if they also reflect a premium paid for other unmeasured unfavorable job characteristics that are correlated with job risk, they may lead one to overstate the true value of life.

Workers' Compensation Benefit Levels and Work Injury Experiences: State Data

In theory, the incidence and duration of work injuries depends on both employee and employer actions. Given the discussion above, this suggests that both the level of benefits *and* the extent of experience rating should affect injury rates. Yet only two empirical studies, to be discussed below, have attempted to evaluate the effects of experience rating. The studies that use statewide data, or industry-by-state data, tend to ignore experience rating and stress the effects of benefit levels alone on the incidence and duration of injuries and/or claims.

The nine studies summarized in table 4.1 fall neatly into three groups. First, there are three studies by James Chelius (1973, 1974, and 1977) that use a single year's data and find that, controlling for other factors, higher workers' compensation benefits are associated with a higher frequency of injury but have no association with duration (severity) of injury. Second, there are two studies by Chelius (1982 and 1983) and one by John Ruser (1985) that use data for a number of years. Chelius (1982) uses data from thirty-six states for the 1972–75 period and finds that higher workers' compensation benefits are associated with more frequent accidents but fewer days per case, so that on balance they have no association with the total rate

TABLE 4.1. Studies of the Relationship between Workers' Compensation Benefit Levels and Injury Rate or Indemnity Claim Frequency and Duration that Use State Data as the Unit of Observation

Study	Data Period and Coverage	Workers' Compensation Benefit Variable	Outcome Variables	Effect of Higher Benefit Levels	Other Workers' Compensation Variables Included (Effect of Increase)
Chelius (1973) Chelius (1974) Chelius (1977)	1967 state-by-manufacturing industry data	Workers' compensation benefit level in the state and industry (actuarial estimates or implied, given average wages, from laws)—weighted average of different types of cases	BLS* Frequency of injury Severity of injury	Increase No effect	—
Chelius (1982)	1972–75 data by manufacturing industries for 36 states	Workers' compensation benefit level in state-industry cell for total temporary injuries divided by average earnings in cell (benefits implied by law given average earnings)	OSHA Frequency rate Days per case Lost workday rate	Increase Decrease No effect	Waiting period (decrease) (no effect) (decrease)
Chelius (1983)	1972–78 data by manufacturing industries for 28 states	(same as above)	OSHA Frequency rate Days per case Lost workday rate	Increase No effect Increase	Waiting period (no effect) (no effect) (no effect)

TABLE 4.1 (*continued*)

Study	Data Period and Coverage	Workers' Compensation Benefit Variable	Outcome Variables	Effect of Higher Benefit Levels	Other Workers' Compensation Variables Included (Effect of Increase)
Ruser (1985)	1972–79 3-digit manufacturing data for 41 states	Average weekly workers' compensation benefit in the state-industry cell for temporary total disability	OSHA Frequency rate of cases Frequency of lost workdays	Increase Increase	Waiting period
Butler and Worrall (1983)	1972–78 data for 35 states	Average weekly workers' compensation benefit in the state for (a) temporary total (b) minor permanent partial (c) major permanent partial injuries (computed from state laws, average wage and assumed wage distributions)	NCCI claim rates for nonself-insuring firms for (A) temporary total (B) minor permanent partial (C) major permanent partial injuries	$\begin{array}{c}\\ a\\ b\\ c\end{array}\begin{array}{\|ccc\|}A & B & C\\\hline 0 & + & +\\ 0 & + & 0\\ 0 & - & +\\\hline\end{array}$	Waiting period (A—decrease) (B—decrease) (C—no effect)
Butler (1983)	15 industries in South Carolina for a 32-year period	Index of average *real* annual workers' compensation payments for various types of injuries	South Carolina Industrial Commission statistics on Lost workday rate Death rate Permanent total rate Permanent partial rate Temporary total injury rate	Increase Increase Increase Increase No effect	

TABLE 4.1 (*continued*)

Study	Data Period and Coverage	Workers' Compensation Benefit Variable	Outcome Variables	Effect of Higher Benefit Levels	Other Workers' Compensation Variables Included (Effect of Increase)
Worrall and Appel (1982)	1958–77 data for the state of Texas	Income-replacement rate for temporary total injuries in the state	NCCI data		—
			Temporary total claims/medical-only claims		
			All indemnity claims/medical-only claims	Increase	
				Increase	

SOURCE: Author's interpretation of material in the original articles. In the Butler and Worrall (1983) row, a " + " indicates increase, a "0" no change, and a "–" a decrease.
*Bureau of Labor Statistics.

of lost workdays. His later study (1983) uses data for only twenty-eight states but a longer period (1972–78) and finds that although the workers' compensation benefit-frequency association is still observed, the benefit–days-per-case relationship vanishes. As a result, higher benefits are associated with an increased total rate of lost workdays. Whether the differences in results between the two studies reflect changes in behavior that occurred in 1976–78 or the dropping of eight states from the sample is not investigated by Chelius.

Finally, Ruser (1985) uses data from forty-one states for the 1972–79 period and finds that higher benefits are associated with higher frequencies of injuries and days lost from work.

Focusing on Chelius (1982), one might ask how higher benefits could simultaneously increase frequency but decrease duration. Unfortunately, there are a number of possible explanations, which the data do not permit us to disentangle. Higher benefits might induce the reporting of minor injuries that otherwise would go unreported and that tend to be of short duration. They might also induce workers to take more risks on the job, but only in situations that would not lead to increased risk of serious long-term injuries. Finally, they might induce employers to concentrate accident prevention resources where long-term injuries are possible, to challenge long-term claims more frequently, or to "encourage" injured workers to return to work more rapidly. Presumably data on workers' compensation claims challenges are available; however, to my knowledge, no researcher has attempted to analyze whether challenges of claims by employers (either at the outset or while a claim is in progress) are related to the level of benefits.

The third group of studies analyzes different types of data. Richard Butler (1983) focused on data from one state, South Carolina, over a long period and found that an index of average *real* annual workers' compensation payments for various injuries in the state was positively associated with the frequency of almost all types of injuries. Butler and John Worrall (1983) used workers' compensation claims data for thirty-five states over the 1972–78 period and computed estimates for each state and year of the levels of various types of benefits. They found benefit levels were associated primarily with permanent partial claims rates, not with temporary total ones. While an increase in the minor (major) permanent partial benefit level was associated with a higher minor (major) permanent partial injury rate, an increase in the major permanent partial benefit level also reduced the incidence of minor permanent partial claims.[12]

This latter result is intriguing in that it suggests that injured workers have some control over how they get their claims classified, whether as a major or a minor injury. Again, there is the possibility that at least part of the observed effect on injury rates may simply be a reporting effect.[13] Evidence to support this view is presented by Worrall and Appel (1982), who found that higher income-replacement rates for temporary total injuries have been associated over time in Texas with an increase in the ratios of temporary total claims and all indemnity claims to medical-only claims.

Similarly, Chelius (1982, 239) found that frequency rates for injuries that involve no lost days appear not to be sensitive to benefit levels; because the waiting period in most states is at least three days, higher benefits offer workers no added incentive to report injuries in this category. He argues that any positive relationship here would indicate a real association between benefits and this short-term injury rate, and this relationship is not observed. Two studies (Chelius 1982 and Butler and Worrall 1983) also found that longer waiting periods are associated with decreased injury rates or claims; whether this is a reporting or a real effect was not ascertained.

Taken together, these studies strongly suggest that increases in workers' compensation benefits are associated with higher injury and claim rates, with at least some fraction of the increase being a pure "reporting" or "classification" effect. They do not, however, provide any strong evidence on duration of claims or injuries, primarily because increased frequency results in changes in the mixture, or types, of injuries reported. To analyze accurately the effects of benefit levels on the duration of claims requires data on individual claims; two such studies are discussed in the next section.

The later studies described in this section are methodologically more sophisticated, controlling for more variables and using more refined data. Nonetheless, their conclusions should probably be tem-

---

12. Major claims are considered more serious than minor ones; the classification depends on the magnitude of the indemnity payment for the injury. This raises the possibility that what is considered a major claim may vary across states.

13. As noted above, Butler and Worrall (1983) find workers' compensation benefits have a larger effect on permanent partial than temporary total claims. The effect on permanent partial claims is unlikely to reflect primarily a reporting effect.

pered for at least two reasons. First, conclusions about the effects of workers' compensation benefits on rates of injuries or injury claims are essentially drawn from observations on the association between benefit levels and injury rates across states or on the association between changes in benefit levels and changes in injury rates over time. Very little concern has been expressed that high injury rates in a state create pressure to have generous benefits or that increases in injury rates create pressure to increase benefit levels. Put another way, there have been only limited efforts (see, for example, Chelius 1974) to test for the possibility that the direction of causation runs from injury rates to benefit levels, rather than vice versa.

Second, the workers' compensation system is a complex system that involves much more than simply specifying the benefit level and waiting period. For example, presumably the extent of experience rating differs across states (and over time) as do administrative stringency in processing claims and the propensity of employers to challenge claims.[14] In contrast to research on unemployment insurance, where these factors have been considered, research on workers' compensation has tended to ignore them.[15] If these variables are correlated with benefit levels, their omission will distort the relationship between the estimated benefit level and the injury rate.

Benefit Levels and the Duration of Claims

Butler and Worrall (1984) and Worrall and Butler (1985) have used data on individual workers' compensation claimants in the state of Illinois to analyze the effects of workers' compensation benefit levels on the duration of temporary total disability claims.[16] The data are confined to one state to control for other aspects of the workers'

---

14. The structure of experience rating is the same across most states at any point in time. The actual extent of experience rating in a state, however, will vary across states with the size distribution of firms, their wage rates, and their prior injury experiences. Hence, in principle, one can compute estimates of the extent of experience rating or of the proportion of firms that are (1) not subject to experience rating or (2) perfectly experience rated and use these in the analyses. There are, of course, obvious econometric problems with this approach.

15. Studies of the effects of administrative stringency in the unemployment insurance literature include Solon 1984 and Horowitz 1977. Studies of the effects of experience rating include Brechling 1981 and Topel 1983.

16. Their research builds on related work for Great Britain by Doherty (1979) and Fenn (1981).

compensation system and to one type of indemnity claim, those arising from low-back injuries, to mitigate the problem of varying mixtures of injury types, found in more aggregate data. The data come from a survey by the National Council on Compensation Insurance (NCCI) of sample claimants in twelve states which began in April 1979 and followed the claimants for forty-two months.

To analyze these data requires estimation methods that take account of the fact that some claimants are still receiving benefits at the end of the forty-two-month period. The two papers use appropriate methods, differing only in the specific stochastic assumptions and assumptions about unobservable variables that they make. These methods have previously been applied to problems of unemployment insurance and unemployment duration, so their papers build directly on research on another social insurance program. (See Flinn and Heckman 1982 and Lancaster 1979, for example.)

Both papers yield the same important result, after controlling for other factors: the higher an individual's income-replacement ratio under the workers' compensation program, the less likely he or she is to leave claimant status and hence the longer the expected duration of his or her claim. A 10 percent increase in benefits is predicted to increase the average duration of a claim by .23 weeks (one day), which represents a 2 percent increase in the lengthening of the average claim (Worrall and Butler 1985). Whether this statistically significant result is large enough to be of "policy significance" is left to the reader to evaluate.[17]

These papers represent, by far, the most sophisticated econometric treatments found in workers' compensation research, and the advantages of using data for a single state and type of injury are evident. Nonetheless, they are not without problems.

In particular, at a point in time in a single state, the income-replacement ratio an individual is scheduled to receive is a negative function of his or her previous earnings. To see why this creates problems, consider how the typical workers' compensation schedule operates. As the top panel of figure 4.1 illustrates, there is a minimum

---

17. They also find that when a lawyer represents a claimant, the duration of the claim is longer. This returns us to the issue of administrative stringency and legal challenges. Their data permit them to analyze some of the influences that determine whether or not a lawyer is used. Another study that addresses this issue is Borba and Appel 1987.

Benefit Levels

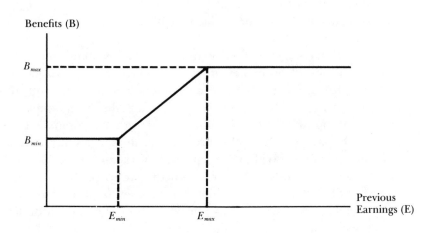

Income-Replacement Ratio

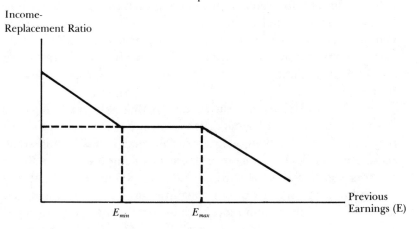

Figure 4.1

benefit level, B_{min}, in the state. If an individual's preinjury earnings fall in the range E_{min} to E_{max}, then benefits increase with earnings. Individuals who previously earned E_{max} or more receive the maximum benefit level in the state, B_{max}. The bottom panel of figure 4.1 shows the implied income-replacement rate (B/E) for this schedule. It is constant (at about two-thirds in most states) between E_{min} and E_{max}; however, outside this region it obviously is negatively related to previous earnings.

If the income-replacement rate for an individual is an exact inverse function of his or her previous earnings, one cannot meaningfully speak of varying the rate at a point in time independently of previous earnings. If both previous earnings and the income-replacement rate appear to influence duration of workers' compensation claims, this may reflect only that previous earnings affect duration in a nonlinear fashion. Without independent variation in the income-replacement rate, we cannot ascertain whether we are really estimating the effect of workers' compensation benefit levels on duration.

Some independent variation may have in fact existed in Butler and Worrall's data.[18] For example, some individuals received lump-sum benefit awards rather than weekly benefits. In these cases, Butler and Worrall divided these amounts by the individuals' *actual* number of claim weeks to obtain a measure of their weekly benefits. This approach causes individuals with claims of randomly long duration to have randomly low reported income-replacement rates. Hence Butler and Worrall tended to *understate* the true effect of workers' compensation benefits on duration. A further problem is that one would expect lump-sum awards to have a different effect on durations of claims than a contingent weekly award. Their approach does not permit this to occur.

The conclusion one reaches here is that although using data from one state has its advantages, it also creates problems. One senses that data from more than one state are needed, although this would require researchers to take other characteristics of the state and state workers' compensation systems into account. Studies of the effect of unemployment insurance benefits on duration of unemployment have used individual data from more than one state, exploiting the interstate variation in replacement rates. (See, for example, Ehrenberg

---

18. This paragraph draws on a telephone conversation with Richard Butler.

and Oaxaca 1976.) The twelve-state NCCI sample is a very useful data base for a similar analysis of workers' compensation. In a recent study, Worrall et al. (1985) used these data and found results that were very similar to the single-state (Illinois) studies.[19]

Experience Rating

In spite of the important role that experience rating plays in determining employers' responses (in theory) to an increase in workers' compensation benefits, there have been only two published attempts to analyze empirically whether experience rating affects injury rates. Chelius and Smith (1983) exploit the fact that small, manually rated firms are not experience rated, while very large firms are perfectly experience rated. The difference between injury rates in small and large firms within a single industry obviously will reflect many factors besides the difference in experience rating. If all else is equal, however, the higher the workers' compensation benefits in a state, the greater, they argue, the incentive faced by large firms in that state to reduce their injury rates, and thus the smaller the difference should be. They test whether experience rating matters by seeing if, across states, higher benefits are associated with lower values of the difference in injury rates between small and large firms in each of fifteen two-digit manufacturing industries. They conclude that their data do not permit them to ascertain any effects of experience rating; if present, the effects are too small to be picked up with the crude data they use.

In contrast, Ruser (1985) appears to find that experience rating matters. He uses the same line of reasoning as Chelius and Smith, but tests the "firm size" hypothesis by using pooled cross-section time-series data for forty-one states from 1972 to 1979 on twenty-five three-digit manufacturing industries. He enters an interaction term between the benefit level and firm size in his injury rate regressions and finds a negative coefficient. He attributes his finding that higher benefits appear to reduce injury rates more in states with larger firms (on average) to the greater likelihood that larger firms will face experience rating.

---

19. Worrall et al. (1985) also use the Illinois data and find that higher benefit levels increase duration more for older workers than for younger ones.

Taken at face value, the results of Chelius and Smith's study suggest that the reduction in injury rates that increasing the extent of experience rating would bring about is so small that policy makers need not worry that many firms face imperfect or no experience rating. In contrast, Ruser's study suggests that increasing experience rating would significantly reduce injury rates. For a number of reasons, one must be cautious, however, in drawing conclusions from either study. The first reason applies to both studies; the latter ones apply only to the Chelius and Smith study.

First, within an industry, benefit levels vary across states, both because of differences in the generosity of state workers' compensation systems and because of interstate differences in average wages. The latter may reflect differences in the mix of skills workers possess. Any observed (or lack of observed) correlation between benefits and injury rate differences between large and small firms across states or between the average size of firms and the correlation of benefit levels and injury rates may reflect the interaction of the skill mix and firm size on injury rates.

Second, average wage differences within a two-digit industry across states may reflect differences in the three- or four-digit industry mix across states, and there is no reason to suppose that the injury rate–firm size relationship is constant across three- or four-digit industries. This makes it difficult (using the Chelius-Smith method) to separate out the effects of workers' compensation benefits from the effects of industry mix.

Finally, average wage differences across states may reflect differences in the wage rate differential between large and small firms within states.[20] If wage rates differ between firms in a state, injury rates may also differ, for reasons completely independent of experience rating.[21]

One senses from all of this that efforts to estimate the effects of experience rating using aggregate state-by-industry data are not likely to prove fruitful, even when the data are stratified by firm size. At first glance, a more promising strategy appears to be to obtain data

---

20. Consider the extreme case in which small firms in every state paid the same wage. A higher average wage in a state would reflect the higher wages paid in large firms and hence the greater wage differential between small and large firms.

21. For example, wage differentials between large and small firms may reflect differences in skills; it is well known that injury rates are related to workers' skills.

at the individual firm level, to impute a marginal workers' compensation cost variable per injury for the firm (using algorithms based on knowledge of the characteristics of the firm and the rules of the experience-rating system) and then to test for the effects of this variable on future injury rates at the firm.[22]

Unfortunately, the marginal cost per injury a firm faces, given its size and wages, will depend on its prior injury rate experience. To the extent that injury rates are correlated over time at a firm, this creates serious statistical problems; it may prove impossible to disentangle the effect of experience rating on injury rates from the effect of injury rates on experience rating. While this effort is worth pursuing, it will require longitudinal data and a careful consideration of statistical issues.

Workers' Compensation and Labor Supply

Several studies have addressed the issue of how permanent partial disability benefits affect labor supply, highlighting the distinction between scheduled and nonscheduled benefits.[23] William Johnson (1983) focused on workers injured in New York State in 1970 who were found eligible for scheduled benefits. These scheduled benefits are specified as weekly amounts for given durations; they are not related to actual wage loss during the period received. Johnson found small effects on the labor supply of benefit levels in 1971, but by 1974 benefit levels appeared to affect neither labor force participation nor hours of work. He suggested that switching to nonscheduled benefits, which are contingent on wage loss, would have the obvious potential to decrease the labor supply.

Some support for this view is found in Burton (1983). Burton used time-series data for New York State from 1959 to 1979 and found that increases in the unemployment rate were associated with a larger number of nonscheduled cases but not with any change in the number of scheduled cases. Workers' compensation payments in the former case are contingent on wage loss, and increases in the

---

22. Victor (1983) has developed such an algorithm.

23. A number of related studies estimate the effect of the Social Security Disability Insurance program on labor force participation rates. See, for example, Haveman and Wolfe 1984a and 1984b, Leonard 1979, and Parsons 1980a, 1980b, and 1984. These studies tend to focus on the labor force participation rates of all older workers, not the rates for a sample of claimants as Johnson does.

unemployment rate make it harder for disabled workers to find jobs that compensate them at the level of their preinjury jobs.

Burton also found, however, that higher benefit levels reduced the number of nonscheduled permanent partial disability cases. While it is possible that this reflects the dominance of efforts by employers to prevent injuries or injury claims over any reduction in actions by employees to promote safety, it must be stressed that this result flies in the face of all of the evidence summarized in table 4.1. Burton's twenty-year time-series analysis does not appear to control for changes in the industry/occupation/age/gender distribution of the labor force, all of which should influence compensation costs and injury rates (see, for example, Dillingham 1983). To the extent that these variables are correlated with changes in benefit levels over time, the observed effect of benefits on nonscheduled claims may actually reflect the effects of these other variables.

Conclusion

A long critical summary of the literature in an area requires no summary; however, several substantive propositions that have relevance for occupational safety and health policies are worth repeating. First, the evidence on compensating wage differentials for risk of injury is nowhere near as solid as producers of the evidence believe. On the one hand, even if we take estimates of differentials at face value and *assume* that all other nonrisk-related conditions of employment have been fully controlled for, the existence of a differential does *not* imply that workers are *fully* compensated for the risk of injury they face. At best, such estimates can be used to provide lower-bound estimates of the "value of life," which in turn can be used in benefit/cost analyses of various occupational safety and health policies. They *cannot* be used to draw conclusions about how well markets are working. On the other hand, if unfavorable nonrisk-related conditions of employment have *not* been controlled for (as is typically the case), and these are positively correlated with injury risk, the estimated wage differentials will overstate the true compensating wage differential for injury risk and thus *may* provide overestimates of the value of life.

Second, higher workers' compensation benefits do appear to increase the frequency-of-injury rates and workers' compensation claims, although we cannot separate out with any precision how much of the increase is "real" and how much is merely a "reporting" effect. If the system is at least partially experience rated (which it is) and labor markets are not perfectly competitive (which they probably are not), higher workers' compensation benefits should induce employers to try to prevent accidents and/or to challenge more claims. That a positive relationship between frequency and benefits is observed implies that employees' responses to higher benefits dominate, on balance, over employers' responses.

The trick, then, is to alter existing policy to increase employers' incentives to improve safety without altering employees' incentives. One possibility is to hold benefit levels at their current real levels but to increase the extent of experience rating. As discussed above, there is no real evidence that this would work, and, in any case, such a policy would be strongly opposed by unions. Increased experience rating increases employers' incentives to challenge workers' claims for benefits. For this very reason, unions have been vocal opponents of attempts to increase experience rating in the unemployment insurance system.

An alternative is to increase the payroll tax but *not* the level of benefits and to use the excess of revenue over benefits to fund other safety and health programs.[24] To the extent that experience rating does matter, this will provide employers with increased incentives to improve safety. Similar proposals have previously been suggested with regard to overtime pay—increasing the tax on overtime hours but not the overtime premium paid to workers—and have been supported by at least some unions.[25]

Of course, the fact that increasing workers' compensation benefits does appear to increase the frequency-of-injury rates and/or workers' compensation claims does *not* imply in itself that further benefit increases are undesirable (*or* are desirable). Rather, it only tells us that there is a trade off between higher, more adequate benefits and higher injury rates and claims. Where along the trade off lines we ultimately locate will depend on policy makers' judgments about the optimal combination of adequacy and safety.[26] For example, the

---

24. Chelius (1982) has previously suggested this.

25. See Ehrenberg and Schumann 1982, chap. 8, for a discussion of these proposals. The United Automobile Workers has been a noted supporter of them.

26. Viscusi and Moore (1987) provide a methodological framework that can be used to help analyze the adequacy of workers' compensation benefits given the wage-

results in Chelius (1983), taken at face value, suggest that raising the income-replacement rate in a state by 10 percent relative to the national average would increase the number of injuries per one hundred full-time workers in a state relative to the national average by 1.6 percent. Whether such an action would, on balance, be desirable is for policy makers to decide.

Finally, it is worth restressing that very little is known about the effects on the frequency and duration of claims of other characteristics of the workers' compensation system, such as administrative stringency, the frequency of employer challenges, and the frequency of the use of attorneys in claims cases. Research on the causes and effects of these other characteristics would clearly help policy makers improve the design of the workers' compensation system.[27]

---

injury rate trade off that exists. Their methodology requires, however, that accurate estimates of the trade off be obtained.

27. Some suggestive evidence on how the benefits to litigating workers' compensation claims vary across states is presented in Butler, Kearl, and Worrall 1984. As noted above, evidence on the variables associated with claimants' hiring of attorneys is found in Borba and Appel 1987 and in Worrall and Butler 1985.

5·LESSONS FOR THE ADMINISTRATION OF WORKERS' COMPENSATION FROM THE SOCIAL SECURITY DISABILITY INSURANCE PROGRAM

Jerry L. Mashaw

The title of this chapter may be misleading in two senses. First, it may suggest that its author thinks he knows enough about the administration of workers' compensation to prescribe solutions for the system's ills. Nothing could be further from the truth. Second, there may be a suggestion of praise for the Social Security Disability Insurance (SSDI) system, which is equally misdirected. While I believe that SSDI is a much better run program than recent press reports would suggest, it is hardly such a specimen of effective administration that its structures and techniques should be transplanted to the soil of workers' compensation systems.

Nevertheless, it may be useful to reflect on some of the perennial issues in workers' compensation administration from the perspective of some years' research on a related but distinct income-support system. The "lessons" that emerge from those reflections are less rules to guide reform efforts than they are puzzles or caveats. They instruct us to pause and consider the perils of prescriptions for highly complex administrative systems.

I cannot here, of course, canvass all the ills of workers' compensation administration or pursue even a short list in great detail. I have chosen, therefore, a set of issues that resonate with problems or experiences in the administration of SSDI. I have called these issues "The Role of Formal Adjudication," "The Role of Settlement," and "The Role of the Claims Examiner." I hope my comparative comments, notwithstanding this peculiar selection process, have greater salience than a discussion I once overheard between an American football fan and a Scots soccer buff. The Scot thought that there was nothing that could not be fixed about the American game—if the officials could only be convinced to change the shape of the ball so that it would bounce properly.

The Role of Formal Adjudication

My initial exposure to the SSDI system was in connection with a study of the hearings and appeals process within the Social Security Administration (SSA) (Mashaw et al. 1978). The hearings process before administrative law judges was at that time in a state of crisis. Requests for hearings were rising steadily; the national percentage of claims granted at hearings was increasing dramatically, although this increase masked vast disparities among the award rates of individual judges; and delays of eighteen months between the time a hearing was requested and the date a decision was rendered were not uncommon. Congressional mailbags were overflowing with complaints from irate SSDI claimants who believed that their cases were being ignored or had been lost in the bureaucratic shuffle.

As my colleagues and I studied the hearings process and how it might be improved, we heard one constant refrain from administrative law judges, "It ain't broke, so don't fix it." The problem, they told us, was not with them but with the underlying administrative process in state agencies. The judges claimed that if the state agency personnel who made initial and reconsideration decisions would just do their jobs properly, there would be no hearings and appeals crisis. Escalating requests for formal hearings, soaring but inconsistent award rates, and unconscionable delays at the hearing stage were merely the visible symptoms of malaise lower down in the decision process.

Similar concerns seem to plague workers' compensation programs (see U.S. Dept. of Labor 1979a, vol. 1). The percentage of cases contested continues to creep up. Claimants who are paid only after formal hearings or litigation encounter enormous problems because of the delays that accompany formal processes. Funds that could be used to provide more adequate benefits are eaten up in process costs, including attorneys' fees. Moreover, the variances in awards made on contested claims seem difficult to explain as reflecting variances in the amounts of wages lost. Given the historic promise of workers' compensation—rapid, noncontentious wage replacement—these facts lead even more easily than in the SSDI system to the conclusion that the substantial use of formal process only reflects some failure in the prior informal process.

Further research on the role of state agencies in the SSDI program and reflection on the relationship between that role and the hearings process, however, have led me to question the notion that the use of formal process is a sign of failure in the informal process, at least in that program. For we must ask what it is reasonable to expect from an informal decision process and whether the social values that are implicit in particular programs can all be served by a noncontentious administrative routine. Indeed, I came to believe that the tension between formal and informal processes in the SSDI program had to be viewed from the much broader perspective of the conflicting social demands on the adjudicatory system and the means by which any such system can maintain its perceived legitimacy (see Mashaw 1983). I fear that I must unpack these ideas in some detail, but they will serve us in the discussion of all three of our proposed topics.

Adjudication and Legitimacy

If one pursues the critical literature on the SSDI system, one finds three well-developed strands of complaints (Mashaw 1983, 21–40). One strand is concerned with the failure of the disability program to provide adequate service to claimants and beneficiaries. This view, at least implicitly, characterizes the program's purposes as paternalistic and therapeutic, purposes that would seem to require a major role in program administration for health care, vocational, social service, and other professionals. The failure of the bureaucratic decision process to emphasize the role of professional judgment and to adopt a service orientation is seen as the program's major deficiency.

A second, more "legalistic" perspective is concerned primarily with the capacity of individual claimants to assert and defend their rights to disability benefits. This literature focuses on such problems as the inadequacy of the notices of denial sent to rejected applicants; the need for representation of claimants in disability hearings; the lack of adversarial testing of the evidence provided by participants in the adjudicatory process; the substantial reversal rate of those cases that are heard orally by independent administrative law judges or are reviewed in federal courts. In sum, the concern is with the failure of the decision process to provide the essential ingredients of judicial trials.

A third strand of the critical literature chides the SSA for failing to manage the adjudication of claims in ways that produce predictable and consistent outcomes. The concern is that the system may be out of control, and the suggestions for reform are essentially managerial: SSA should provide more complete and objective criteria for the exercise of adjudicatory discretion; greater control should be gained over the internal routines of the disability decision services in the states; the system of management oversight and statistical quality assurance should be strengthened. In short, the system is viewed as a bureaucracy and criticized for its inadequate management controls.

In reflecting on these patterns, I have come to some hypotheses that seem to have interesting implications, not just for the disability program but for the evaluation of administrative adjudication generally. First, these criticisms reflect distinct conceptual models of administrative justice. Second, each of the models is coherent and attractive. But, third, the models, while not mutually exclusive, are highly competitive: the internal logic of any one of them tends to drive the characteristics of the others from the field as it works itself out in concrete situations.

The three strands in the critical literature on the disability program suggest three arguments about justice: (1) that decisions should be accurate and efficient concrete realizations of the legislative will; (2) that decisions should provide appropriate support or therapy from the perspective of relevant professional cultures; and (3) that decisions should be arrived at fairly when assessed in the light of traditional processes for determining individual entitlements. Elaboration of these arguments in the context of the disability program produces three distinct models of administrative justice; I have called these models *bureaucratic rationality, professional treatment,* and *moral judgment.*

Bureaucratic Rationality

Given the democratically (legislatively) approved task—to pay disability benefits to eligible persons—the administrative goal in the ideal conception of bureaucratic rationality is to develop, at the least possible cost, a system for distinguishing between true and false claims. Adjudication should be both accurate (the legislatively specified goal) and cost-effective. This approach can be stated more broadly by introducing trade offs between error, administrative, and other "process" costs such that the goal becomes "minimize the sum of error and other associated costs."

A system focused on correctness defines the questions presented to it by making decisions in essentially factual and technocratic terms. Individual adjudicators must be concerned about the facts in the real world that relate to the truth or falsity of the claimed disability. At a managerial level the question becomes technocratic: what is the least-cost methodology for collecting and combining those facts about claims that will reveal the proper decision?

The general decisional technique, then, is information retrieval and processing. And, of course, this application of knowledge must in any large-scale program be structured through the usual bureaucratic routines: selection and training of personnel, detailed specification of administrative tasks, specialization and division of labor, coordination via rules and hierarchical lines of authority, and hierarchical review of the accuracy and efficiency of decision making. In the disability program, for example, decision making goes on not in one head but, initially, in the heads of thousands of state agency examiners.

From the perspective of bureaucratic rationality, administrative justice is accurate decision making carried on through processes appropriately rationalized to take account of costs. The legitimating force of this conception flows both from its claim to correct implementation of otherwise legitimate social decisions and from its attempt to realize society's preestablished goals in some particular substantive domain while conserving social resources for the pursuit of other valuable ends. No program, after all, exhausts our conception of good government, much less of a good society or a good life.

Professional Treatment

The goal of the professional is to serve the client. An administrative system for disability decision making based on professional treatment would, therefore, be client oriented. It would seek to provide those services—income support, medical care, vocational rehabilitation, and counseling—that the client needed to improve his or her well-being and perhaps regain self-sufficiency.

Like bureaucratic rationality, professional judgment requires the collection of information that may be manipulated in accordance with standardized procedures. But in the professional treatment model, the incompleteness of facts, the singularity of individual contexts, and the ultimately intuitive nature of judgment would be recognized, if not exalted. Disability decisions would be viewed not as attempts to establish the truth or falsity of some state of the world, but rather as prognoses of the likely effects of disease or trauma on functioning and as efforts to support the client while he or she pursues therapeutic and vocational prospects.

An administrative system for providing professional treatment would thus have characteristics rather different from those of the system supporting bureaucratic rationality. The basic idea would be to apply the appropriate profession to the problem at hand. And because these allocation decisions—decisions about needs or ability to help—are themselves professional judgments, they would be made best by the relevant professionals in conjunction with claimants. Administration would include the facilitation of these contacts, co-ordination of multiprofessional teams, and implementation of professional judgments concerning particular cases. Substantive and procedural rules, hierarchical controls, and considerations of efficiency would all be subordinated to the norms of the professional culture. The organization would be more a lateral network than a hierarchical command structure.

The basis for the legitimacy of professional treatment is in one respect similar to that of bureaucratic decision making: the professional is master of an arcane body of knowledge and supports his or her judgment by appeals to expertise. But whereas the bureaucrat displays his or her knowledge through instrumentally rational routines designed to render transparent the connection between concrete decisions and legislatively validated policy, the professional's art remains opaque to the layperson. The mystery of professional judgment is, nevertheless, acceptable because of the service ideal of professionalism. Justice lies in having the appropriate professional judgment applied to one's particular situation in the context of a service relationship.

Moral Judgment

To some degree the traditional notion of justice in civil and criminal trials implies merely getting the facts right in order to apply existing legal rules. So conceived, the goal of a moral judgment model of justice is the same as that of a bureaucratic rationality model—factually correct realization of previously validated legal norms. If this conception exhausted the notion of adjudicatory fairness, competition between moral judgment and bureaucratic rationality would entail merely a technical dispute about the most efficient way to find facts. But there is more to the competition than that.

The moral judgment model views decision making as value defining. The question is not just who did what, but who is to be preferred, all things considered, when interests, and the values to which they can be relevantly connected, conflict.

This entitlement-awarding goal of the moral judgment model gives an obvious and distinctive cast to the basic issue for adjudicatory resolution. The issue is the deservingness of some or all of the parties in the context of certain events, transactions, or relationships that give rise to a claim. This issue, in turn, seems to have certain implications with regard to a just process of proof and decision. For example, the fair disposition of charges of culpability or lack of desert requires that claims be specifically stated and that any affected party be given an opportunity to rebut or explain allegations. For this contextualized exploration of individual deservingness to be meaningful, the decision maker must be neutral—that is, not previously connected with the relevant parties or events in ways that would impair the exercise of independent judgment on the evidence and arguments presented.

The goals of this most traditional model of justice may suggest additional decisional techniques and routines designed to preserve

TABLE 5.1. Features of the Three Models of Justice

Dimensions/ Model	Legitimating Values	Primary Goal	Structure or Organization	Cognitive Technique
Bureaucratic rationality	Accuracy & efficiency	Program implementation	Hierarchical	Information processing
Professional treatment	Service	Client satisfaction	Interpersonal	Clinical application of knowledge
Moral judgment	Fairness	Conflict resolution	Independent	Contextual interpretation

party equality and control, promote agreed allocations, and protect the authority of the decider. But these are details that need not detain us. The important point is that the "justice" of this model inheres in its promise of a full and equal opportunity to obtain one's entitlements. Its authority rests on the neutral development and application of common moral principles within the contexts giving rise to entitlement claims.

Comparison

As we have described them, each model of justice is composed of distinctive goals, specific approaches to framing the questions for administrative determination, basic techniques for resolving those questions, and subsidiary processes and routines for decision making that functionally describe the model. The distinctive features of the three models are outlined in table 5.1. These features are, of course, meant to indicate the central tendencies, not to suggest that features and whole models do not shade one into another at the margins.

Although the SSDI program began with a vision that attempted to combine all these models of justice, it has by now become stratified into a lower-level (state agency) bureaucratic process that is highly routinized and objective and a subsequent hearing process that is highly individualized, contextual, and judgmental. Both processes consider claims de novo. Although doctors and vocational experts offer evidence and advice in both processes, and eligibility for disability insurance carries with it eligibility for Medicare, the program is not closely tied to any therapeutic regime or to attempts to rehabilitate or to reemploy workers.

From one perspective the incidence of SSDI hearings and the high level of "disagreement" of administrative law judges with prior decisions (administrative law judges on average grant 50 to 60 percent of the claims they hear) are not implicit criticisms of the state agency process. The two processes are doing different things. The state agencies rapidly process a very high volume of claims at a very modest cost on the basis largely of "objective" medical indicators. Through the force of regulations, those medical criteria readily classify cases into the critical categories: wholly disabled from performing any job available in substantial numbers in the national economy or not as disabled. SSA physicians assign "residual functional capacity" scores when necessary wholly on the basis of clinical findings in the case file. To be sure, this impairments-oriented process oversimplifies claimants' situations. For most claimants, however, eligibility would not be altered by a more comprehensive analysis of their situation.

The hearings process is performing a quite different function. Here the cases are developed much more fully to take account of individual responses to pain and illness. The complex effects of multiple impairments on energy levels, the complications of psychological overlays and environmental limitations, the imponderables of intelligence, experience, and motivation—all can be explored through live testimony and personal observation. A decision can be reached "all things considered" whether this particular claimant should be expected to continue to work. This process is designed to render essentially moral judgments in cases that elude objective classification, or for claimants who believe that they do.

If we take this two-function view of the SSDI process, then it is highly likely that reforming one level of the process to make it more like the other will also make it less good at performing its unique function. A more subjective and judgmental informal process will also be slower and less accountable for its accuracy. A speedier and more objective (and presumably therefore more consistent) hearing process will be less individualized, contextual, and, from one perspective, just. These trade offs are inevitable absent a willingness to make vastly larger investments in the administrative process for determining eligibility for SSDI or some great (and currently unknown) leap forward in decisional technology. The SSDI hearings and appeals crisis of the

1970s thus may only have reflected an influx of aggressive claimants and/or marginal cases into the system as a result of a variety of environmental changes—rising unemployment, the growth of knowledge about the system, and the availability of free legal services, to name but a few.

Turning to the world of workers' compensation, one might at least ask whether increased contentiousness there is not a function of some of these same variables. Contested cases appear most frequently, after all, in the permanent disability cases that are most similar to SSDI claims. In these cases, workers' compensation resembles a pension rather than a compensation system and operates on murky criteria that often are reminiscent of the SSDI standard. It may be that one simply cannot expect these cases to be adjudicated out of the system swiftly, correctly, and without dispute. Eliminating contention without simultaneously impairing the perceived "fairness" of the decision process might be accomplished only by fundamentally reorienting the substantive criteria for awards to eliminate all "judgmental" elements.

The Role of Settlement

Settlement is, of course, closely related to the Anglo-American notion of formal hearing. In common-law jurisdictions, trial implies adversary presentation and party control of proceedings. Party control in turn implies the power to terminate the formal process by settlements or compromise.

Yet, settlement seems peculiar when public programs create entitlements to income support. Beneficiaries are considered to have legal rights that do not conflict with the public interest. Program administrators have a duty to pay all eligible claimants and a corollary duty to withhold payment when eligibility is not demonstrated. Resolving disputes by settlement suggests adversary interests and malleable or problematic claims—ideas foreign to the ideology of modern positive programs of income support.

Commentators who view workers' compensation from this latter perspective are thus concerned about the propriety of lump-sum settlements of workers' compensation claims. Lump-sum settlements threaten both the adequacy and equity ideals of workers' compensation systems. There is growing evidence that workers accept compromise payments that undervalue their claims and that the settlements made from case to case fail to reflect the true worth of individuals' entitlements. Both the *Report of the National Commission on State Workmen's Compensation Laws* (1972, 109–10) and the *Report of the New York Temporary State Commission on Workers' Compensation and Disability Benefits* (1986, 36–59), for example, take a very dim view of lump-sum settlements.

Yet, however appealing the case for moving workers' compensation schemes in the direction of assured pensions to replace lost wages, the experience in true pension systems, such as SSDI, suggests caution. Much of the delay and apparent inconsistency in that system seem to be a direct result of the inability to compromise or settle claims that are inherently judgmental and, therefore, contestable. In SSDI, to be sure, there need be no concern with the claimant who "settles" for too little. But for that worry is substituted the nagging suspicion that the real difference among many claims pressed to and paid after the formal hearing stage lies not in the strength of the claim but in the knowledge or aggressiveness of the claimant. Moreover, because cases are judgmental and are dominated by issues of fact, the administrative law judge functions rather more like a single-member jury than a judge. The inevitable consequence is extreme variance in outcomes. Awards often appear to be as much a function of who heard the case as a result of its intrinsic merit.

As my colleagues and I have suggested elsewhere (Mashaw et al. 1978), these unhappy features of the "all-or-nothing" SSDI system are quite resistant to reforms in the process. Very large increases in administrative costs would be necessary to ameliorate these problems without simultaneously creating others of equal or greater magnitude. Indeed, we were often attracted by the idea of settlements—perhaps disguised as permanent partial awards—as a way of lessening the adjudicatory tensions that plague SSDI.

Hence, when confronted with proposals to reduce the possibility of a settlement in workers' compensation, I am at best skeptical. If the claims involved cannot be resolved on some quasi-objective basis, then they are inherently contestable. If contestable or problematic, these claims will produce competing visions of the "truth" that are irreconcilable. Maintaining the legitimacy of the decisional apparatus then requires the availability of formal processes for contesting claims. And for that formal process to work efficiently, the opportunity for settlement may be a practical necessity. Indeed, unless all settlement opportunities are removed from the system, one might expect that problematic claims would be classified in ways that maintained the possibility for settlement, and thus for speedy and inexpensive disposition.

Settlement is surely not ideal. It may be viewed as a historic artifact of the tort system that should be banished from a modern workers' compensation program. But unless compensation is made on a purely objective basis, banishing settlement will probably leave problems of equity, adequacy, and timeliness that are at least as troubling as is the settlement process itself.

The Role of the Claims Examiner

The inefficiencies of formal hearings and the inequities of the settlement process might both be avoided were it possible to structure the benefits of the professional treatment model of administration into the workers' compensation system. Indeed, the claims examiner, whether retained by a compensation carrier, a state agency, or an employer, is sometimes described as an all-purpose professional facilitator. In theory at least, the claims examiner guides the claimant through the process of filing a claim, makes referrals for medical care and vocational rehabilitation, monitors the efficacy of treatment, and provides continuity of therapy and income support from the time of inquiry to return to work. Interview data on claimants' perceptions suggest that the theoretical possibilities are not being realized in most cases. But the question remains: might it be possible to eliminate contentiousness, settlements, and formal hearings, while retaining legitimacy, through a restructuring of the role of the claims examiner to emphasize the ethics of professional service?

The experience in the SSDI program again suggests that, while incremental improvements are surely possible, a restructuring of the mode of treatment is hardly a panacea. Indeed, the original idea for administering that program—delegation of the eligibility-determining function to state vocational rehabilitation personnel to be integrated with state rehabilitation efforts—has proved a complete failure. The poor fit between the categories—not disabled for purposes of SSDI and good candidate for vocational rehabilitation—puts the SSDI program and state vocational rehabilitation professionals hopelessly at odds. The service or treatment culture cannot be maintained when the professional must deny both a pension and rehabilitation services to a substantial portion of the population. State agencies quickly found it necessary to separate eligibility for SSDI and rehabilitation functions. Today there is little operational connection between the two activities.

SSDI has also had difficulty accommodating the medical culture in its decision process. Treating physicians are often conservative in their advice and reports. The SSA has adopted regulations making it clear that a treating physician's conclusion that a claimant "cannot work" is not to be viewed as evidence in the claims process. Only the physician's clinical findings are probative, and even they must be interpreted by SSA personnel (sometimes consulting physicians) to make them useful for claims adjudication. The physician, like the vocational rehabilitation counselor, has been found unsuited to the specific tasks of determining SSDI eligibility.

The usual workers' compensation claims examiner, an adjuster employed by a compensation carrier or an employer, seems equally unsuited to the service tasks described earlier. The adjuster, like the physician and the rehabilitation counselor, is oriented to a different goal. Operating within the general milieu of property and casualty claims, the adjuster's purpose is to provide least-cost disposition of claims. Moreover, the adjuster must to some degree monitor the reasonableness of the costs imposed by providers of medical and other therapeutic services. In this context, devotion primarily to the claimants' service and support needs can hardly be expected.

Reform in the mode of treatment would therefore entail something like complete removal of the claims-examining function from the property and casualty claims-adjustment context, perhaps by putting claims examination in a separate state agency. But that would hardly be enough. The existing practice of state agencies seems only modestly distinguishable from the practice of private insurers. Data on differences in the treatment of claims (e.g., U.S. Dept. of Labor 1979b, 3:65–90) seem to suggest that *where* a claim arises matters more than what type of coverage (private insurance, self-insured, or state scheme) the employer carries.

There is obviously a serious problem of bureaucratic control involved in the claims examination process. An attempt to mandate a service orientation would confront the enormous difficulties of monitoring and directing the activities of a corps of street-level bureau-crats. Only some very basic parameters of their activities, such as timeliness and cost control, would be measurable. The service activities that give promise to the treatment-oriented ideal would be obscured from the view of all but the claims examiner and the claimant.

In short, in this situation the only guarantee of effort and competence is likely to be a professional culture. But no profession other than some variant of social work seems to fit the requirements. Indeed, given the range of skills involved, one would seem to need a doctor, lawyer, rehabilitation specialist, counselor, and accountant rolled into one. Perhaps such a professional can be created by appropriate training and acculturation. And, if created, perhaps we would trust that professional with the allocation of workers' compensation dollars.

I confess that I remain doubtful. The SSDI program was unwilling to adopt the treatment culture of the physician or vocational rehabilitation specialist. Moreover, when it did create a new profession—the so-called vocational expert who testifies in administrative law hearings concerning the availability of jobs for which a claimant might be suited—it gave that profession only an advisory and evidentiary role that could be controlled almost completely by the real decision maker, the administrative law judge. My published suggestions (Mashaw et al. 1978, 205–9) that SSDI experiment further with multiprofessional panels have generated hardly a flicker of interest.

The distrust of professionals by SSDI administrators is motivated largely by cost-consciousness; it is likely to hit a resonant chord with those concerned about the costs of workers' compensation. Moreover, if comparisons were made with another income-support program, Aid to Families with Dependent Children, one would find a similar distrust and abandonment of program administration by professional social workers, premised there on the fear of coerciveness that may be bred when the profession's paternalistic aims are combined with control over the clients' income (see Simon 1983). The professional treatment model thus seems unlikely to dominate benefits administration in workers' compensation programs or elsewhere.

Conclusion

Lest my ruminations appear either a counsel of doom or, at best, a Panglossian defense of the status quo, let me reiterate my purpose. I have meant only to bring to bear in a limited way such insights as were gained in my studies of the SSDI program. The lesson that most impressed me there was the extraordinary complexity involved in designing systems that can keep multiple and competing objectives in tolerable balance while they are administered by human beings. I am thus skeptical that every reform proposal may represent merely an idea that has not been tried lately and, therefore, whose costs have been forgotten. My skepticism is nevertheless exuberant. Nothing should be unthinkable just because everything is, in some sense, unworkable. In the end we can make even marginal gains only by risking the inevitable failure of every reform either to improve all dimensions of administration simultaneously or to honor fully each of our competing visions of just adjudication.

6 ·THE FUTURE OF WORKERS' COMPENSATION

Robert J. Lampman and Robert M. Hutchens

Workers' compensation is our first social insurance program. It dates from 1908, when a forerunner of the Federal Employees Compensation Act was passed, and from 1911, when the first state programs were adopted. Workers' compensation today exists in each of the fifty states, the District of Columbia, and Puerto Rico. Federal legislation gives workers' compensation protection to federal employees and to longshore and harbor workers and protection similar to workers' compensation to railroad and maritime employees and coal miners. Close to 90 percent of all employees are covered by workers' compensation and similar programs, all of which provide cash benefits, health care, and rehabilitation services in response to work-related injuries and disease.

The history of workers' compensation has not been one of steady growth. During several of its first seven decades, it languished or stagnated. In the 1970s, however, in response to pointed prodding by the federal government, workers' compensation exhibited a vibrant capacity to grow. Some other social welfare expenditure programs have grown more spectacularly in recent decades. Some of these, most notably federal disability insurance and private group health insurance, have grown up alongside workers' compensation and seem to offer clear alternatives to the protection workers' compensation offers against the loss of income and the cost of health care associated with work-related injuries and illness. Hence, on the one hand, it is not hard to imagine that the roles of workers' compensation could be taken over by other, perhaps federal, programs.

On the other hand, it may be that workers' compensation will have another burst of growth like that of the 1970s, with emphasis on new risks to workers from radioactive and toxic materials, or with attention to some aspects of nonoccupational disability. To get perspective on the alternative futures of workers' compensation, it is helpful to look first at its present role and then at its past.

Workers' Compensation as Part of a Broad Set of Social Welfare Expenditure Programs

In 1978, state and federal workers' compensation programs paid out $5.9 billion in cash benefits and $3.8 billion in health care benefits. This $9.7 billion equaled 0.5 percent of the gross national product (GNP) in that year. All social welfare expenditures under public programs equaled 18.1 percent of GNP, which indicates that workers' compensation is a relatively small program. Workers' compensation looks even smaller if we broaden the definition of social welfare expenditures to include private expenditures mediated by pension funds, group insurance, or philanthropic organizations and those funded by certain interfamily direct gifts. This broader definition yields a ratio of what can be called secondary consumer income (SCI) to GNP of 27.6 percent for 1978. (See table 6.1 and appendix tables A.1–A.4.) The latter four tables indicate the broad range of benefits that may be used by disabled persons and their families. Cash benefits and health care benefits, which are most relevant to a discussion of workers' compensation, amounted to 19.5 percent of GNP. (See panel C of table 6.1.)

The $5.9 billion of cash benefits paid out under workers' compensation in 1978 were about one-eighth of the $48.1 billion paid out in cash for disability in that year by all public and private programs. These include Social Security Disability Insurance (SSDI), supplemental security income (SSI), temporary disability insurance, veterans' compensation, workers' compensation, and group disability benefits and paid sick leave. (See table 6.2, panel A.)

The medical benefits of workers' compensation, which were $3.8 billion in 1978, were a very small part of all the public and private expenditures for health care that contributed to secondary consumer

TABLE 6.1. Secondary Consumer Income (SCI) Benefits

Item	1978 (% of GNP)
A. Total SCI benefits	27.6
B. Benefits by intermediary	
Government	19.6
Insurance	3.4
Philanthropy	0.6
Interfamily	4.0
C. Benefits by type	
Cash	13.9
Health care	5.6
Education	5.2
Food, housing, and other welfare services	2.9
D. Benefits by population category	
Age 62 and older	9.5
Disabled, under age 62*	3.8
Female family head, with children	2.2
All others	12.1
E. Sources of SCI funds, by type	
Taxes	
Total	18.0
Payroll†	6.6
Property	1.6
State general revenue	4.2
Federal general revenue	5.5
Wage diversion	4.7
Philanthropy	0.6
Interfamily	4.0

Sources: Lampman 1984, tables 4.2, 4.3, and 4.5. Corrections were made to panel D to include new information for lines 10 and 18 in table A.1 herein.

*Benefits assigned to this group include those paid out by disability insurance, SSI (for disabilities only), workers' compensation, and veterans' compensation. They also include private group disability and paid sick leave benefits, part of Medicare and other health programs, a per capita share of education, and a part of food, housing, and other welfare services. The disabled under age 62 are about 5% of the population aged 16 to 61. They received 14% of all SCI benefits in 1978 (Lampman 1984, table 5.4). Berkowitz (1985, 37, table 3) presents what he calls "total disability expenditures" in 1978 equal to 3.5% of GNP.

†Includes workers' compensation premiums.

TABLE 6.2. Workers' Compensation Benefits and Other Selected
Public and Private Benefits Related to Disability and Health Care,
1978 (in billions of dollars)

	Workers' Compensation	Other Public Benefits	Private Benefits
A. Cash benefits			
Workers' compensation	5.9		
Disability insurance		12.8	
Supplemental security income		4.6	
State and railroad temporary disability insurance		1.1	
Veterans' compensation		8.0	
Group disability benefits and paid sick leave			15.7
SUBTOTAL	5.9	26.5	15.7
B. Health care benefits			
Workers' compensation	3.8		
Other public benefits (including Medicare and Medicaid)		72.1	
Group insurance			42.3
Philanthropic expenditures			2.2
SUBTOTAL	3.8	72.1	44.5
C. TOTALS	9.7	98.6	60.2

SOURCES: Tables A.1 and A.2.

income. In that year, government-mediated health care (including
that covered by workers' compensation) amounted to $75.9 billion,
and private group health insurance companies amounted to $42.3
billion. (See table 6.2, panel B.) Medical benefits from workers' compensation, then, were only about 3 percent of all health care benefits
under public and private transfer arrangements.

A rather different question is how workers' compensation figures in the set of all public and private transfers that are received by
those classified as disabled. Table 6.1, panel D, shows that about 14
percent of all secondary consumer income benefits, that is, $83 billion
or 3.8 percent of GNP in 1978, go to those families headed by a
nonaged but disabled person. The calculation starts with programs
clearly targeted at the disabled, such as SSDI, SSI, workers' compen-

sation, and vocational rehabilitation, and then adds benefits that are more broad based but that can be claimed by families of the disabled, such as education. This calculation does not take account of all social welfare benefits that may go to disabled persons and their families, however. No effort was made to divide interfamily direct gifts to show those related to disability. (See lines 11 and 29 in table A.1 and line 17 in table A.4.) Nor was any effort made to take account of the fact that those who experience a disability undoubtedly substitute one public or private cash benefit for another. Thus early retirement benefits may be an alternative to a disability claim under workers' compensation. Or dependents of a disabled worker may seek a benefit from the Aid to Families with Dependent Children (AFDC) program. Still, the $9.7 billion of workers' compensation benefits is a substantial share of the above noted $83 billion of secondary consumer income benefits that go to families headed by nonaged but disabled individuals.

Other authors have undertaken to answer this question concerning the relative importance of workers' compensation. Thus Richard V. Burkhauser and Robert A. Haveman (1982) present what they call a "disability system," including SSDI, SSI, workers' compensation, and other targeted public programs, which paid out $70.4 billion in cash and health care benefits in 1977. These benefits went to about 10.8 million disabled persons, and the per capita benefit was between $6,000 and $10,000. They also list another forty-two programs that pay some benefits to the families of disabled persons, although they are not especially aimed at the disabled. AFDC, for instance, paid one-fifth of its benefits to such families. These forty-two programs paid $23 billion to the disabled. The combined sets of programs delivered $93.4 billion worth of benefits to disabled persons in 1977.

Monroe Berkowitz, William G. Johnson, and Edward H. Murphy (1976, 24–38 and table 3.1) set forth a statement of what they call a workers' disability income system. They identify eighty-five separate public and private programs that delivered cash and health care and related benefits in the amount of $83 billion in 1973. Berkowitz (1985) and Berkowitz and M. Anne Hill (1986, 5, table 1) present a similar social accounting scheme with a total expenditure for disability of $76 billion in 1978, $98 billion in 1980, and $122 billion in 1982. They include such items as outlays for vocational rehabilitation and part of AFDC benefits. They also include $6 billion of indemnity payments under liability insurance for negligence leading to automobile accidents, medical malpractice, and miscellaneous bodily injuries. In this connection, it is interesting to note that the net premiums paid to property and casualty companies for automobile liability insurance were $26 billion in 1982; premiums for medical malpractice were $1.5 billion (Insurance Information Institute 1983, 16). It is also interesting that nearly half of product liability litigation is workplace related (National Legal Center for the Public Interest 1981, 9).

There are both gaps and overlaps in the disability system. Some disabled persons or their survivors are simultaneously eligible for two or more programs, the benefits of which are not fully integrated. Thus a worker may draw a benefit from workers' compensation and a benefit from the tort system and a Social Security benefit and a veteran's benefit (Johnson 1979). At the same time, some disabled persons are not eligible for benefits under any program. This is particularly true for short-term, nonwork-related disabilities, which are covered only by private insurance and temporary disability insurance in five states. We estimate that the share of the national total of income lost due to disability that is replaced by organized secondary consumer income programs is not much above 25 percent. This is true in spite of workers' compensation's nominal replacement rate for short-term disability of 67 percent. The 25 percent ratio is about the same as that for unemployment but substantially below the near 50 percent ratio for income loss due to retirement and probably below that for the loss of a family breadwinner.

In sum, the $9.7 billion in cash and health care benefits paid out by workers' compensation in 1978 looks small in relationship to GNP and to the substantial benefits paid out by public and private institutions in the form of social welfare expenditures or secondary consumer income. It looks considerably larger in relationship to the total benefits paid to the disabled, which are variously estimated to have been in the range of $70 to $93 billion in 1978. And it must be larger still when related to the part of the $70 to $90 billion public and private benefits that is responsive only to work-related injuries and illness.

The Relative Growth of Workers' Compensation since 1950

Rough estimates cited above are that workers' compensation mediated one-eighth of the cash benefits for disability and 3 percent of all health care benefits that were part of secondary consumer income in 1978. What has happened to these ratios over time? Has workers' compensation kept up with the rapid increase of public and private secondary consumer income? The ratio of total secondary consumer income to GNP rose from 17.2 percent in 1950 to 27.6 percent in 1978. That 60 percent increase in the overall ratio was not uniform across all classifications of benefits and sources of funds. Health care benefits grew much faster than other benefits, and benefits targeted for the disabled, along with those for the aged and female heads of families, increased more than benefits for people outside those three groups.

Table 6.3, panel A, shows that between 1950 and 1980 cash benefits from workers' compensation (line 7) increased at the same rate as total public and private cash benefits for disability (line 2). Benefits of private group disability and paid sick leave plans grew twice as fast as workers' compensation benefits (line 8). Table 6.4 shows that cash disability benefits grew at a faster rate than all cash benefits for retirement, disability, loss of breadwinner, unemployment, and other risks combined. The ratio of 1980 benefits to 1950 benefits shows that cash benefits for disability increased 23.9 times while all cash benefits increased "only" 14.5 times. (In the same period GNP increased 9.2 times.) Table 6.5 shows that between 1950 and 1978 the number of beneficiaries of workers' compensation increased fourfold, while the number of beneficiaries of some other selected cash benefit programs increased even faster.

Health care benefits from workers' compensation in 1980 were 18.5 times as great as in 1950 (table 6.3, panel B), but that ratio is well below the ratios found for the other secondary consumer income benefits for health care and well below the ratio for the total (32.9). The most dynamic of the health programs was private group insurance with a ratio of 52.2. From table 6.3 we can conclude that cash benefits from workers' compensation grew along with other cash benefits for disability, but workers' compensation benefits were rather slow followers in the fast track of health care expenditures.

Reasons for Growth in Workers' Compensation Benefits, 1950–80

This section focuses on growth in benefits under the regular state workers' compensation programs. It excludes consideration of the federal black lung program, which began in 1969 and paid out $1.7

TABLE 6.3. Workers' Compensation Benefits and Other Selected Benefits Related to Disability and Health Care (in billions of dollars)

	1950	1960	1970	1978	1980	1982	1980/1950
A. Cash Benefits							
1. Total (includes 2)	26.8	56.4	116.2	301.7	389.9	473.5	14.5
2. Disability (includes 3–8)	2.8	6.8	17.5	48.1	67.0	78.2	23.9
3. Disability insurance	—	0.7	3.5	12.8	15.6	17.3	22.3*
4. Supplemental security income (disability only)	0.1	0.3	1.0	4.6	5.4	6.7	54.0
5. State and railroad temporary disability insurance	0.1	0.4	0.7	1.1	1.4	1.8	14.0
6. Veterans' compensation	1.7	2.8	4.5	8.0	9.4	11.2	5.5
7. Workers' compensation (includes survivors)†	0.4	0.9	2.0	5.9	9.6	12.2	24.0
8. Private group disability and paid sick leave	0.5	1.7	5.8	15.7	25.6	29.0	51.2
B. Health Care Benefits							
1. Total (includes 2 and 4)	4.5	11.8	40.9	120.4	148.1	191.6	32.9
2. All government (includes 1–3)	3.3	6.8	25.4	75.9	98.2	128.3	29.7
3. Workers' compensation	0.2	0.4	1.0	3.8	3.7	4.7	18.5
4. All private (includes 5 and 6)	1.2	5.0	15.5	44.5	49.9	63.3	41.6
5. Group insurance	0.9	4.5	14.5	42.3	47.0	60.0	52.2
6. Philanthropy	0.3	0.5	1.0	2.2	2.9	3.3	9.7

SOURCES: Tables A.1 and A.2.
*Ratio for 1980 to 1960.
†Data for 1984 are at panel A, line 7, $13.2 billion; at panel B, line 3, $6.4 billion (Price 1986).

TABLE 6.4. Secondary Consumer Income Cash Benefits, Grouped by Risk, 1950–80, and Ratios of 1980 to 1950 (in billions of dollars)

Risk	1950	1980	1980/1950
Total	26.8	389.9	14.5
Retirement	6.2	187.6	30.3
Disability	2.8	67.0	23.9
Loss of family breadwinner	1.3	23.5	18.1
Unemployment	2.6	29.6	11.4
Other	13.9	82.2	6.4
GNP, fiscal year	286.5	2633.1	9.2

SOURCE: Table A.1.

billion in benefits in 1980. Growth in benefits under the regular workers' compensation programs is a consequence of demographic and economic trends as well as program changes. To isolate the different factors, it is especially useful to view growth in the cash benefits of the regular programs as a product of trends in four variables: (1) the number of wage and salary workers in the economy; (2) the average earnings of workers covered by workers' compensation; (3) the percentage of covered wage and salary workers in the economy; and (4) expenditures on these compensatory benefits as a percentage of covered payrolls. Expenditures on these compensatory benefits are equal to the product of these four variables, as is demonstrated in the notes to table 6.6. The first two variables influence expenditures but are primarily determined outside the program, while the latter two variables are largely determined by program coverage and payment rules. This decomposition helps us examine the extent to which growth in expenditures arises from forces that are beyond government control.

Table 6.6 presents the relevant data. It is clear that outside forces played an important role in program growth. Between 1950 and 1980 the work force almost doubled, and average earnings of covered workers more than quadrupled. (Also see Dillingham 1983.) These variables do not, however, explain the full extent of the growth. Between 1950 and 1980 the percentage of wage and salary workers covered by workers' compensation increased from 77 percent to 88 percent, and benefits as a percentage of payrolls almost doubled, from .36 to .70. Indeed, even if the work force and average earnings had not changed between 1950 and 1980, expenditures would have more

TABLE 6.5. Beneficiaries of Selected Consumer Income Cash
Benefit Programs and Ratios of 1978 to 1950

Benefit	Number of Beneficiaries (millions)		1978/1950
	1950	1978	
Retirement			
OASDHI*	1.9	21.8	11.5
Railroad retirement	0.2	0.6	3.0
Federal employee retirement	0.2	1.9	9.5
State and local retirement	0.2	2.0	10.0
SSI (aged only)	2.8	2.0	0.7
Private pensions	0.5	9.1	18.2
Disability			
OASDHI	—†	4.9	—†
Veterans' programs	2.3	3.3	1.4
Federal retirement	0.1	0.5	5.0
State and local retirement	0.0	0.2	6.7
SSI (blind and disabled)	0.3	2.2	11.0
Workers' compensation	0.3	1.3	4.3
Loss of family breadwinner			
AFDC	2.2	10.6	4.8
OASDHI (survivors' insurance)	1.1	7.6	6.9
Unemployment			
Unemployment insurance	1.4	2.0	1.4
General assistance	0.9	0.8	0.9

SOURCE: *Social Security Bulletin, Annual Statistical Supplement* (1980), table 13,
150, and 174–77. Private pension numbers from Munnell 1982, 11. Workers' compensation number for 1950 is from Somers and Somers 1954.
*Old age survivors', disability, and health insurance.
†Program did not exist.

than doubled because of changes in coverage and benefits as a percentage of payrolls.[1]

Since coverage increased relatively little over the 1950–80 period, most of this "program effect" is due to growth in benefits as a
percentage of payrolls. And most of that growth occurred in the 1970–
80 decade. In fact, the data suggest that were it not for the 1970–80
growth in benefits as a percentage of payrolls, 1980 expenditures

---

1. C/W grew by a factor of 1.13 and X/P by a factor of 1.91. If W and P/C
did not change, then expenditures would have grown by a factor of $1 \times 1 \times 1.13 \times 1.91 = 2.16$. See table 6.6 for an explanation of terms.

TABLE 6.6. Cash Benefits in Workers' Compensation Regular Programs

Year	Cash Benefits* (in millions of dollars) (X)	Wage/Salary Workers (in millions) (W)	Payroll per Covered Worker (P/C)	Percentage of Wage/Salary Workers Covered (C/W)	Benefits as a Proportion of Payrolls (X/P)
1950	$415	47.7	$3098	77.2	.00364
1960	$860	55.9	$4900	80.4	.00391
1970	$1871	70.6	$7449	83.8	.00424
1980	$7909	90.9	$14,416	87.6	.00696
			Ratio of Later Year to Earlier Year		
1950–60	2.07	1.17	1.58	1.04	1.07
1960–70	2.18	1.26	1.52	1.04	1.08
1970–80	4.23	1.29	1.94	1.05	1.64
1950–80	19.06	1.91	4.65	1.13	1.91

SOURCE: Derived from Price 1984a, tables 1 and 3.
*Note that $X = W \times (P/C) \times (C/W) \times (X/P)$.

would have been $4.8 billion rather than $7.9 billion.[2] Other sources indicate that the most rapid growth occurred in the four years following the 1972 report of the National Commission on State Workmen's Compensation Laws.[3] After 1976, benefits as a percentage of payrolls grew at a more gradual rate. The most recent data (Price 1986) indicate this slower rate has continued into the 1980s.

There are two possible reasons for this rise in expenditures as a percentage of payrolls: (1) an increase in the number of compensable cases per covered worker and (2) growth in benefits per compensable case that exceeds growth in earnings per covered worker.[4] Some rather rough evidence suggests that the first reason is not very important. There was apparently only a slight increase in compensable cases per covered worker between 1950 and 1980 (Price 1984, tables 4 and 5). The second reason is evidently the critical one. Benefits per compensable case increased more rapidly than the average earnings of covered workers, implying greater earnings replacement under the program. Thus at least part of the growth in the compensatory component of expenditures was due to improvements in the benefits paid to injured or diseased workers.

Growth in the medical and hospitalization component of workers' compensation benefits can be decomposed in a similar fashion. Consider the following four variables: (1) the number of wage and salary workers in the economy; (2) the price index of medical goods and services from the consumer price index (1967 = 100); (3) the percentage of covered wage and salary workers in the economy; and (4) real workers' compensation medical benefits per covered worker (denominated in 1967 dollars). As before, it can be shown that medical and hospitalization expenditures are equal to the product of these

2. Were it not for the 1970–80 growth, X/P would have grown by a factor of 1.16 over the period (.00424/.00364 = 1.16). Then 1950–80 expenditures would have grown by a factor of $1.91 \times 4.65 \times 1.13 \times 1.16 = 11.60$, and 1980 expenditures would be $.415 \times 11.6 = $4.8 billion.

3. See Price 1984, table 5. Other evidence is consistent with this. For example, Burton and Krueger (1986) present evidence on the cost of workers' compensation to employers that suggests a slower rate of growth toward the end of the decade. Moreover, compliance scores on nineteen recommendations of the national commission increased more rapidly between 1973 and 1976 than between 1977 and 1980. See U.S. Department of Labor 1985.

4. $X/P = [(X/CC)/(P/C)][(CC/C)]$ where X/P = expenditures on compensatory benefits as a percent of payrolls; X/CC = expenditures on compensatory benefits/number of compensable cases; P/C = average earnings (see text); and CC/C = number of compensable cases/number of covered workers.

four variables. The first two variables are again essentially beyond the control of program administrators, while the latter two are at least in part determined by program rules and regulations.

Table 6.7 presents data on the variables. Clearly, part of the growth in medical benefits is due to a growing work force and the rising cost of medical care, both of which are essentially outside the control of the government. That, however, is only part of the story. Much as was the case for the compensatory component of expenditures, even if these two variables had not changed between 1950 and 1980, medical expenditures would have more than doubled because of increases in coverage and real medical benefits per covered worker, variables that are in part determined by program rules and regulations. Note also the rather steady growth in real medical benefits per covered worker. Unlike the data on compensation expenditures, the data here give no evidence that the 1970s represent a sharp break with the past.

Much of the growth in workers' compensation benefits between 1950 and 1980 was attributable to forces that were largely beyond the control of program administrators, such as price inflation, work force growth, and rising earnings. Program changes did, however, play a role. The share of the work force protected by the program rose from 77 percent to 87 percent over the period. Medical and cash benefits also increased relative to covered payrolls, with growth in case benefits being particularly important in the 1970s.

The program changes that contributed to expenditure growth were apparently incremental. Before 1972, these changes often took the form of increased maximum weekly benefits for temporary total disability or increased total time and money limits on medical coverage. (See "Workmen's Compensation Payments and Costs" 1958, 1963, and 1970.) After 1972, the states moved to meet the criticism of the national commission by raising maximums, improving permanent partial benefits, moving to blanket or full coverage of occupational disease,[5] and eliminating restrictions on medical care (Price 1979). Although important and expensive, these changes were incre-

---

5. During the 1970s, many states changed their laws so as to provide "full coverage" for work-related diseases. There remain, however, significant barriers to obtaining benefits. For example, many states place a limit on the time period between exposure to a hazard and the manifestation of a disease. For further details, see Crum and Forester's Occupational Disease Task Force 1983. Also see Barth 1980.

TABLE 6.7. Medical and Hospitalization Benefits in Workers' Compensation Programs

Year	Medical and Hospitalization (in millions) (MX)*	Wage/Salary Workers (in millions) (W)	Medical Price Index (MPI)	Percentage of Wage/Salary Workers Covered (C/W)	Real Medical Expenditures per Covered Worker (MX/MPI × C)
1950	$200	47.7	53.1	77.2	$10.12
1960	435	55.9	79.1	80.4	12.25
1970	1050	70.6	120.6	83.8	14.71
1980	3893	90.9	265.9	87.6	18.58
Ratio of Later Year to Earlier Year					
1950–60	2.18	1.17	1.47	1.04	1.21
1960–70	2.41	1.26	1.52	1.04	1.20
1970–80	3.71	1.29	2.20	1.05	1.26
1950–80	19.47	1.91	4.95	1.13	1.84

Source: Derived from Price 1984, tables 1 and 3. Medical Price Index from U.S. Department of Commerce 1984, table 789.
*MX = W × MPI × (C/W) × (MX/MPI × C).

mental in the sense that they did not represent a fundamental shift in the objectives of workers' compensation.

What were the underlying political forces that promoted change in the program? The available literature often emphasizes interest groups.[6] Labor unions and employer associations have historically been major actors in determining the content of workers' compensation legislation. While playing lesser roles, the insurance industry and the legal profession are also important. According to the national commission, these interest groups can sometimes exercise a virtual veto over changes in the law:

> In some States, the legislatures have reacted to complexities by in effect delegating authority for workmen's compensation to important interest groups. Under the "agreed bill" procedure, legislatures adopt amendments mutually acceptable to labor and management. Unfortunately, these parties often deadlock: employers block action because they object to cost increases associated with general improvements in the law; trade unions because they will not surrender certain cherished practices, such as the right to a de novo trial, which labor in some States considers an important element of protection. (National Commission 1972, 124)

One might speculate that benefit growth is most likely in states where employer associations are weak relative to organized labor or where the several interest groups perceive "reform" to be in their common interest.

From this point of view, the 1950–70 period was characterized by a kind of balance of interest group forces in the states. In some states, the labor movement was sufficiently effective to push through incremental program changes (e.g., increased maximums). In other states, employer associations succeeded in minimizing such changes and thereby holding down costs. Evidence that tends to support this conjecture comes from recently presented data on average adjusted "manual rates" between 1950 and 1972 in twenty states (Burton and Krueger 1986, table 15). The average adjusted manual rate is essentially a measure of workers' compensation insurance costs as a percentage of payrolls for a fixed distribution of industries; it reflects the influence of experience rating, premium discounts, and dividends. To illustrate, Burton and Krueger find that the manual rate in Illinois

---

6. See the five papers on previous reform efforts in National Commission 1973. Also see J. A. Thompson 1979 and 1980 and Berkowitz and Berkowitz 1985.

rose from .437 percent of payroll in 1950 to .657 percent in 1972. For the twenty states, we calculate there is a +.36 correlation between the proportion of the labor force that belonged (in 1960) to unions and the change in manual rates between 1950 and 1972. Thus states where unions represent a large proportion of the labor force tended to exhibit a large increase in that period in workers' compensation costs as a percentage of payroll. This is at least consistent with the notion that benefit growth between 1950 and 1970 in part reflects the political effectiveness of labor unions in a few states.

By 1970 this balance of forces was upset by the federal government. Particularly important was the 1969 enactment of the Federal Coal Mine Health and Safety Act:

> This "Black Lung" legislation partially reflects the historically inadequate coverage of occupational diseases in some State laws.... It is apparent that the Federal government is making substantial effort to rectify the inadequate occupational disease coverage in prior workmen's compensation statutes. (National Commission 1972, 52)

The image of an interventionist federal government was reinforced by the Occupational Safety and Health Act of 1970, which created a new role for the federal government in accident prevention and also set up the National Commission on State Workmen's Compensation Laws. In its 1972 report, the national commission concluded that "State Workmen's Compensation laws were in general neither adequate nor equitable" (1972, 25) and that

> congressional intervention may be necessary to bring about the reforms essential to survival of the State Workmen's Compensation System. We believe that the threat of or, if necessary, the enactment of Federal mandates will remove from each State the main barrier to effective workmen's compensation reform: the fear that compensation costs may drive employers to move away to markets where protection for disabled workers is inadequate but less expensive. (National Commission 1972, 27)

There are other reasons the threat of federal intervention might have been effective. Insurance companies may have wished to avoid federal regulation or even an eventual federal takeover of part of their business. (This had happened with the Medicare program in 1965.) Employers may have fought federal intervention because of its ultimate effect on costs or the possibility of losing immunity from tort liability. By this interpretation, during the early 1970s employers and insurance companies may have been willing to cooperate with the labor movement and improve the existing workers' compensation program in order to forestall federal intervention. Growth in benefits as a percentage of payrolls may have slowed in the latter part of the 1970s because the likelihood of federal intervention had diminished.

Of course, this is too brief a treatment of thirty years of history. Legislation depends not only on interest groups but on public opinion, the economic environment, and the adroitness of political actors. An analysis that focuses on interest groups does, however, seem to possess a degree of explanatory power.

Possible Futures for Workers' Compensation

Workers' compensation was designed early on to occupy a certain space among programs that respond to disability. That space is defined as work-related disability. Workers' compensation compromised the interest workers have in a prompt and adequate remedy and the interest employers have in protection against unpredictably high costs. It sought via experience rating to enlist the employer in action to prevent accidents and to rehabilitate workers. It grew up as a state program in an era when the federal government played only a limited role in social welfare programs. The design and theory of workers' compensation has meant that it could not easily be expanded to cover the costs of nonwork-related disabilities.

The delicate compromise that is workers' compensation has been sustained even though the federal role in disability programs has grown substantially, with Aid to the Permanently and Totally Disabled (APTD) in 1950 and its successor, SSI, in 1972; with SSDI, which was introduced in 1956 and substantially amended in later years; and with Medicare and Medicaid in 1965. The federal government assumed the leadership role in preventive work with the Occupational Safety and Health Act in 1970 and invaded state territory in providing workers' compensation benefits with the Coal Mine Safety Act of 1969 and the Black Lung Benefits Reform Act of 1977. A similar incursion into the territory of workers' compensation was signaled by the Rehabilitation Act of 1973, which increased the federal role in regulating the treatment of the handicapped by governments and employers. Moreover, the decades since 1950 have seen the rapid growth of health care benefits provided by private group health insurance and a continued growth of private group disability insurance and paid sick leave programs that supplement cash benefits from workers' compensation.

Prospects of Decline

While workers' compensation once stood alone in a well-defined space, it now is only one of several occupants in a crowded arena of overlapping programs. Each part of its design is currently being challenged, and it is not clear that it will survive. Can the states continue to fend off possible effects on workers' compensation of the growing federal role in social welfare policy? It is notable that the role of the federal government has not been constricted by the workers' compensation theory that dictates separate financial arrangements for work-related disabilities. Will the justification for a special program for work-related disabilities be denied by the trend toward cash benefits and health care for all who suffer a disability without regard to cause? Is court challenge to workers' compensation as the exclusive remedy for a work-related disability going to lead to a new overarching national system of no-fault insurance that erases the lines between work and nonwork causes of accident and disease and between employer and product liability? (See Larson pp. 21–43 in this volume.) Is federal legislation needed to ensure benefits to workers who suffer from long-latency conditions such as asbestosis? Will insurance premiums for workers' compensation be replaced by a national payroll tax as the general method of funding disability benefits?

Workers' compensation's struggle for survival goes on in the courtroom and at the collective bargaining table as well as in legislative halls. It also continues in academic circles where evaluators seek to quantify the social costs and social benefits of alternative programs for disability. Here harsh questions are put to empirical test. For example, does experience rating as practiced really induce accident prevention by the employer? Because the costs of workers' compensation to a firm can depend on the firm's injury experience, it was originally thought that the program would encourage firms to reduce the frequency and severity of on-the-job accidents. By 1950, several authorities were questioning whether the program actually had this effect (Somers and Somers 1954, 228–35). These doubts persisted over the next three decades (see Worrall 1983). In addition, some experts began to argue that workers' compensation may actually discourage safety; by promising benefits in the event of injury, it may discourage workers from behaving in a careful manner (see Ehrenberg pp. 71–96 in this volume).[7] Thus the 1950–80 period would seem to have been characterized by increasing doubt as to whether workers' compensation can play an effective role in preventing accidents. Passage of the 1970 Occupational Safety and Health Act could be viewed as a political and legislative manifestation of this changed perception.

Scholars have also questioned whether workers' compensation and private health insurance drive up the cost of health care and whether generous cash benefits encourage workers to withdraw from the labor force. Regarding the latter question, Sheldon Danziger, Robert Haveman, and Robert Plotnick (1981) concluded that cash benefit programs for disability, including SSDI and workers' compensation, may have caused the current labor force to be as much as 1 percent smaller than it would otherwise be. Unfavorable answers to these and similar questions undercut support for workers' compensation and perhaps also for its private supplementation.

Given such challenges, it is possible that workers' compensation will decline, with other programs taking over its different roles. For example, the national commission raised (and dismissed) the possibility of assigning

> permanent total disability cases to the Disability Insurance (DI) program of Social Security and temporary total disability cases to State temporary disability insurance (TDI) programs. The medical component of workmen's compensation could be assigned to an expanded Medicare or national health insurance program, and rehabilitation could be absorbed by the State Departments of Vocational Rehabilitation (DVR). Finally, the safety aspects could be assumed by the enforcement agencies of the Occupational Safety and Health Act of 1970. (National Commission 1972, 120)

The main argument for such plans is that they would eliminate the distinction between occupational and nonoccupational disability. Proponents claim that the distinction is untenable because the problems

---

7. See Kasper 1975 and Chelius 1977 for proposed reforms or alternatives to workers' compensation that would restore some aspects of tort liability.

disability causes as regards economic security are the same regardless of whether that disability arises on or off the job. Moreover, they claim that because the distinction is fraught with ambiguity, it leads to needless litigation and costly administration.

Workers' compensation would also decline if a new federal program were introduced that eliminated the distinction between occupational and nonoccupational disability. In fact, New Zealand moved in this direction in 1974 by introducing a government no-fault program as a substitute for a system of accident compensation that primarily relied on workers' compensation and personal injury suits. The program compensates not only work-related injuries but also injuries that arise out of automobile accidents, medical practice, and criminal acts. Similarly, social insurance programs for the temporarily and permanently disabled in the Netherlands do not distinguish between on- and off-the-job disabilities. Interestingly, the ratio of cash benefits for disability to GNP is much higher in the Netherlands than in the United States. That ratio was 2.5 percent in the United States in 1980 and 1982 (see line 12 in table A.1), while it was 7.2 percent in the Netherlands in 1981 (calculated by the authors from Ministry for Social Affairs and Employment 1982 and related government documents).

Yet plans that would eliminate the distinction between occupational and nonoccupational disabilities have not gained political momentum in the United States. This is perhaps because their critics find serious problems with them. For example, the national commission pointed out that programs like SSDI or state temporary disability insurance do not deal with permanent partial impairments. These benefits account for a major portion of all cash benefits in workers' compensation. The national commission asked whether a more comprehensive program would eliminate this form of coverage for workers.

A similar problem arises for health care. One might think that the health care benefits of workers' compensation could easily be taken over by voluntary health insurance, which now covers more than three-fourths of all employees. It would, however, probably require strong legislative intervention to bring such benefits up to present workers' compensation standards, which generally deny deductibility, co-payment, and benefit maximums provisions. Substituting any program for any part of workers' compensation is thus likely to have some opposition.

Indeed, because of this political opposition, we believe that decline in workers' compensation is unlikely in the near future. The workers' compensation program has a natural constituency. Every state and congressional district presumably contains employers, insurance company representatives, attorneys, and unions who perceive benefits from its continued operation. A plan that in the name of efficiency and equity would assign the several functions of workers' compensation to other programs, especially without protection of the employer from tort liability, lacks a similar constituency. The longevity of the workers' compensation program attests to its political viability.

Prospects for Expansion

Workers' compensation encompasses federal or state programs that provide cash benefits, health care, and rehabilitation services in response to work-related injuries and disease. Here we will consider expansions of workers' compensation that remain within those bounds. As such, an increase in the coverage of short-term nonoccupational disability through programs such as temporary disability insurance does not constitute an expansion of workers' compensation, even if the programs are administered by the Workers' Compensation Board.

Rapid expansion of workers' compensation could conceivably occur through a broader response to occupational illness. Particularly salient in this regard are illnesses with long latency periods such as those associated with coal dust, asbestos, and radiation. (In this regard, see Sunshine 1980.) Although the regular state programs have historically changed at a glacial pace in this area, during the 1970s the black lung program grew rapidly. If the problem of occupational illnesses with long latency periods becomes more acute, and if the regular state workers' compensation programs do not move to address it, there could be an expansion of workers' compensation through new federal programs.[8] Expansion of the regular state program could

---

8. Were this to happen, the black lung program would probably not serve as a model for such federal programs. After completing a detailed review of the program, Barth (1987, 277) states that "the greatly enlarged scope of the black lung program

perhaps also be a result of federal standards regarding illnesses of long latency (for example, standards that assign liability to one or more employers or that liberalize requirements that benefits must be claimed within a short time after exposure to a hazard). Yet, even in the activist 1970s, defenders of the state programs were able to block this kind of intervention. Thus, in our view, such federal standards are unlikely. A more likely source of rapid expansion would be new federal programs that address occupational illness.

Perhaps, however, the most likely scenario is for workers' compensation to grow in much the same way that it did during the 1950–80 period. Workers' compensation would then remain part of a pluralistic system of disability programs. It would maintain its unique role in providing cash benefits for permanent partial disability and a shared role with respect to permanent total disability and temporary disability. Workers' compensation would also share the program space for health care benefits, accident and disease prevention, and rehabilitation. This scenario can include long periods of slow growth such as occurred between 1950 and 1970 or periods like the 1970s when the program's objectives remained essentially unchanged but expenditures grew rapidly as states moved to fend off federal initiatives. It could also include adaptation by the states to new federal programs for occupational and environmental illness similar to the black lung program, as well as to new tensions between workers' compensation and tort law and to changes in private health and disability insurances. Under this scenario workers' compensation would continue to grow at about the same pace as other disability programs.

Conclusion

Workers' compensation exhibits striking vitality. At its inception in the early twentieth century, it stood virtually alone as a program for the disabled. Now it is surrounded by an array of programs that deal with various aspects of disability, including income loss, medical care, accident prevention, and rehabilitation. Yet, between 1950 and 1980, cash benefits for workers' compensation grew at a rate equal to that of all cash disability programs combined. While some state programs

---

together with its many perceived difficulties, appears to have strengthened the hand of state program supporters."

that were born in the early twentieth century have either withered away or are now dominated by the federal government (e.g., mothers' pensions), workers' compensation largely remains the state-operated program envisioned by its founders.

In thinking about the future of workers' compensation, two themes seem particularly important. First, workers' compensation is being challenged on several fronts. This challenge takes the form of federal, state, and private safety and disability programs that intrude into the traditional territory of workers' compensation. It also takes the form of academic research that raises harsh questions about the impact of workers' compensation on such varied phenomena as injury rates, labor supply, and price inflation. All of these challenges could serve to erode support for workers' compensation. Workers' compensation is still unique, however, in supplying certain benefits to workers—particularly cash benefits for permanent partial disability—and in providing employers immunity from negligence claims under tort law.

A second theme is the political viability of the regular state programs. These programs share a natural constituency. Every state and congressional district presumably contains employers, insurance company representatives, attorneys, and unions who perceive benefits from their continued operation. Even during the activist 1960s and 1970s, defenders of the state programs were able to mobilize against and ward off federal standards. Given this, it seems unlikely that other programs or new programs will step in and take over the historic role of the state programs.

Thus, looking to the future, we find good reason to expect workers' compensation programs to continue as part of an expanding pluralistic response to the problem of disability.

Appendix

TABLE A.1. Secondary Consumer Income Cash Benefits, Grouped by Risk (in billions of dollars)

Benefit	1950	1960	1970	1978	1980	1982
1. Total (lines 2 + 12 + 19 + 23 + 27)	$26.8	$56.4	$116.2	$301.7	$389.9	$473.5
2. Retirement (lines 3–11)	6.2	20.9	49.7	142.0	187.6	246.3
3. Old age insurance	0.5	8.0	19.3	58.7	75.7	104.9
4. Survivors' insurance (aged)	0.1	1.1	3.8	13.3	17.2	23.5
5. Supplemental security income (aged) or old age assistance	1.4	1.8	1.9	2.6	2.8	3.1
6. Public employee retirement	0.8	2.6	8.6	29.9	39.5	50.1
7. Railroad retirement	0.3	0.9	1.6	4.0	4.8	5.8
8. Veterans' pensions	0.4	0.6	0.9	1.7	1.9	2.1
9. Additional income tax exemptions for aged and blind and credit for the elderly	0.7	1.0	1.3	2.2	2.5	2.8
10. Private pensions*	0.5	1.8	5.9	15.7	25.7	29.0
11. Interfamily (aged)	1.5	3.1	6.4	13.9	17.5	25.0
12. Disability (lines 13–18)	2.8	6.8	17.5	48.1	67.0	78.2
13. Disability insurance	0.0	0.7	3.5	12.8	15.6	17.3
14. Supplemental security income or aid to blind and disabled	0.1	0.3	1.0	4.6	5.4	6.7
15. State and railroad temporary disability insurance	0.1	0.4	0.7	1.1	1.4	1.8
16. Veterans' compensation	1.7	2.8	4.5	8.0	9.4	12.2
17. Workers' compensation	0.4	0.9	2.0	5.9	9.6	11.2
18. Private group disability and paid sick leave	0.5	1.7	5.8	15.7	25.6	29.0
19. Loss of family breadwinner (lines 20–22)	1.3	2.8	8.6	20.5	23.5	25.2
20. Survivors' insurance (children present)	0.2	1.2	3.1	7.4	8.8	10.1
21. Aid to Families with Dependent Children	0.6	1.1	5.0	12.5	14.0	14.4
22. Veterans' life insurance	0.5	0.5	0.5	0.6	0.7	0.7

TABLE A.1 (*continued*)

Benefit	1950	1960	1970	1978	1980	1982
23. Unemployment (lines 24–26)	2.6	3.5	6.0	24.1	29.6	30.6
24. Unemployment Insurance and Employment Service†	2.3	3.1	3.9	12.7	18.3	21.7
25. General and emergency assistance	0.3	0.3	0.6	1.5	1.7	2.0
26. Other public aid‡	0.0	0.1	1.5	9.9	9.6	6.9
27. Other (lines 28–30)	13.9	22.4	34.4	67.0	82.2	93.2
28. Exemptions for children under 18	6.5	9.7	8.4	11.9	12.8	12.1
29. Earned income tax credit	—§	—	—	0.1	0.5	0.6
30. Interfamily (nonaged)	7.4	13.4	26.0	55.0	68.9	80.5

SOURCES: Lines 3, 4, 13, and 20 are derived from the *Social Security Bulletin, Annual Statistical Supplement* 1982, 105–7. The *Statistical Supplement* presents data for calendar years so these were adjusted to a fiscal-year basis and checked against the fiscal-year totals for OASDHI, shown in Bixby 1981, 4, and for 1980 in Bixby 1983, 10. Lines 5 and 14 are derived from the *Statistical Supplement* 1982, 4, 225, 247–49. SSI replaced old age assistance and aid to the blind and disabled in 1974. Lines 6, 7, 15, 16, 21, 23, and 25 are from Bixby 1981, 4, and for 1980 from Bixby 1983, 10. Lines 8 and 16 appear as a combined total in Bixby 1981, 4, and for 1980 from Bixby 1983, 10, but were divided with 17% going to pensions and the remainder to compensation. Lines 9, 28, and 29 are from Lampman 1984, table A.7. Lines 10 and 18 appear as a combined total in McMillan and Bixby 1980, 15, but were divided with 50% going to pensions and 50% to group disability and paid sick leave. This division was guided by study of Chamber of Commerce 1983, tables 4, 20, and 21. Lines 11 and 30 are from Lampman 1984, table A.6. Lines 20 and 24 are derived from the *Statistical Supplement* 1982, 247 (table 188), and 249 (table 190). The calendar year data were adjusted to a fiscal-year basis and checked against the fiscal-year totals for public assistance in Bixby 1981, 4, and Bixby 1983, 10, for 1980.

*Includes benefits for loss of breadwinner and unemployment.

†Includes railroad unemployment insurance.

‡Work relief, other emergency aid, surplus food for the needy, repatriate and refugee assistance, temporary and emergency assistance, and work experience training programs under the Economic Opportunity Act and Comprehensive Employment and Training Act.

§Program did not exist.

TABLE A.2. Secondary Consumer Income Benefits for Health Care, by Funding Source (in billions of dollars)

Benefit	1950	1960	1970	1978	1980	1982
1. Total (lines 2 + 15 + 16)	$4.5	$11.8	$40.9	$120.4	$148.1	$191.6
2. Government (lines 3–14)	3.3	6.8	25.4	75.9	98.2	128.3
3. Medicare	—	—	7.2	25.2	35.0	50.4
4. Medicaid	0.1	0.5	5.2	20.4	27.4	34.4
5. Hospital and medical care	1.2	2.9	5.3	10.7	12.2	15.0
6. Veterans' health and medical care	0.6	0.9	1.7	4.9	5.8	7.8
7. Workers' compensation	0.2	0.4	1.0	3.8	3.7	4.7
8. Vocational rehabilitation (health care only)	0.0	0.0	0.1	0.3	0.3	0.3
9. State temporary disability insurance (health care only)	0.0	0.0	0.1	0.1	0.1	0.1
10. Maternal and child health	0.0	0.1	0.4	0.7	0.8	0.9
11. School health	0.0	0.1	0.3	0.4	0.6	0.7
12. Other public health facilities	0.4	0.4	1.4	5.0	6.8	8.5
13. Medical facilities construction	0.5	0.6	1.0	2.5	2.8	2.6
14. Income tax deductions for medical expense (tax savings)	0.3	0.9	1.7	1.9	2.6	2.9
15. Group insurance	0.9	4.5	14.5	42.3	47.0	60.0
16. Philanthropy	0.3	0.5	1.0	2.2	2.9	3.3

SOURCES: Lines 3–13 are from Bixby 1981, 4.

Line 14 is from Lampman 1984, table A.7, line 6.

Line 15 includes Blue Cross, Blue Shield, independent group plans, and group insurance by insurance companies. Line 15 is from *Social Security Bulletin* (June 1977), 15, for 1950–75, and *Health Care Financing Review* (Sept. 1981), 75, for calendar year 1978.

Line 16 is from Lampman 1984, table A.5.

TABLE A.3. Secondary Consumer Income Benefits for Education, by Funding Source (in billions of dollars)

	1950	1960	1970	1978	1980
1. Total (lines 2 + 8)	10.1	19.7	55.2	113.2	134.4
2. Government	9.4	18.0	51.6	106.1	125.2
3. Elementary and secondary	5.6	15.1	38.6	73.2	86.8
4. Higher	0.9	2.2	9.9	21.9	26.1
5. Vocational and adult	0.2	0.3	2.1	6.1	7.4
6. Veterans' educational benefits	2.7	.4	1.0	3.4	2.4
7. Basic Education Opportunity grants	—*	—*	—*	1.5	2.5
8. Philanthropy	0.7	1.7	3.6	7.1	9.2
9. Elementary and secondary	0.4	0.8	1.2	2.6	3.2
10. Higher and postsecondary	0.3	0.9	2.4	4.5	6.0

SOURCES: Lines 3–6 are from Bixby 1981, 4.

Line 7 is from U.S. Department of Education 1981, 10.

Lines 9 and 10 are from table A.5.

*Program did not exist.

TABLE A.4. Secondary Consumer Income Benefits for Food, Housing, and Other Welfare Services, by Funding Source, 1950–80 (in billions of dollars)

Benefit	1950	1960	1970	1978	1980
1. Total (lines 2 + 16 + 17)	$8.0	$12.7	$26.1	$62.6	$83.2
2. Government (lines 3–15)	2.8	6.0	15.2	41.1	56.4
3. Food stamps	—	—	0.6	5.1	9.1
4. Child nutrition	0.2	0.4	0.9	3.6	5.3
5. Public housing	0.0	.1	0.5	3.6	4.6
6. Other housing	0.0	0.0	0.2	1.6	2.0
7. Income tax savings on owner-occupied housing	1.4	4.6	8.6	16.3	22.2
8. Veterans' welfare services	0.9	0.2	0.4	0.8	0.9
9. Public assistance social services	—	—	.7	2.8	2.3
10. Vocational rehabilitation (excluding medical)	0.0	0.1	0.5	1.0	1.0
11. Institutional care	0.2	0.4	0.2	0.4	0.5
12. Child welfare	0.1	0.2	0.6	0.8	0.8
13. Income tax saving on child care and dependent care expense	—	—	0.2	0.6	0.9
14. Special OEO and ACTION programs	—	—	0.8	0.9	0.9
15. Social welfare not elsewhere classified	0.0	0.0	1.0	3.6	2.3
16. Philanthropy	0.7	1.1	2.0	4.3	5.2
17. Interfamily for food and housing	4.5	5.6	8.9	17.2	21.6

SOURCES: Lines 3–6, 8–12, 14 and 15 are from Bixby 1981, 4, and Bixby 1984.
Lines 7 and 13 are from Lampman 1984, table A.7, lines 8–9.
Line 16 is from Lampman 1984, table A.5, line 6.
Line 17 is from Lampman 1984, table A.6, line 7.

BIBLIOGRAPHY

American Medical Association, Committee on Rating of Mental and Physical Impairment
    1971   *Guides to the Evaluation of Permanent Impairment.* Chicago: AMA.

Arnould, Richard, and Nichols, Len
    1983   "Wage-Risk Premiums and Workers' Compensating Age Differentials." *Journal of Political Economy* 91 (April):332–40.

Baroody, William J., Jr.
    1985   "America: A Nation of Communities." *Memorandum* 45 (Spring/Summer):4–5.

Barth, Peter S.
    1980   "Some Recent Evidence on the Extent of Occupational Disease in Workers' Compensation." (Mimeo.)
    1981   "Compensation for Asbestos-Associated Disease: A Survey of Asbestos Insulation Workers in the United States and Canada." In *Disability Compensation for Asbestos-Associated Disease in the U.S.* New York: Environmental Sciences Laboratory, Mt. Sinai School of Medicine.
    1983   "A Proposal for Solving the Problems of Compensating for Occupational Disease." Paper presented at the Workers' Compensation Conference, Orono, Maine, July 12.
    1987   *The Tragedy of Black Lung: Federal Compensation for Occupational Disease.* Kalamazoo, Mich.: W. E. Upjohn Institute for Employment Research.

Berkowitz, Edward D.
    1979   ed., *Disability Policies and Government Programs.* New York: Praeger.

Berkowitz, Edward D., and Berkowitz, Monroe
    1984   "The Survival of Workers' Compensation." *Social Sciences Review* 58 (June):260–80.
    1985   "Challenges to Workers' Compensation: An Historical Analysis." In *Workers' Compensation Benefits: Adequacy, Equity, and Efficiency,* edited by John D. Worrall and David Appel, 158–79. Ithaca, N.Y.: ILR Press.

Berkowitz, Monroe
  1985a   "An Overview of the Economics of Disability." (Mimeo.)
  1985b   "Disability Expenditures, 1970–1982." New Brunswick, N.J.: Bureau of Economic Research, Rutgers University. (Mimeo.)
Berkowitz, Monroe, and Burton, John F., Jr.
  1987   *Permanent Disability Benefits in Workers' Compensation.* Kalamazoo, Mich.: W. E. Upjohn Institute for Employment Research.
Berkowitz, Monroe, and Hill, M. Anne
  1986   "Disability and the Labor Market: An Overview." In *Disability and the Labor Market*, edited by Monroe Berkowitz and M. Anne Hill, 1–28. Ithaca, N.Y.: ILR Press.
Berkowitz, Monroe, Johnson, William G., and Murphy, Edward H.
  1976   *Public Policy toward Disability.* New York: Praeger.
Bixby, Ann K.
  1981   "Social Welfare Expenditures, Fiscal Year 1979." *Social Security Bulletin* 44 (November):3–12.
  1983   "Social Welfare Expenditures, Fiscal Year 1980." *Social Security Bulletin* 46 (November):3–13.
  1984   "Social Welfare Expenditures, 1981 and 1982." *Social Security Bulletin* 47 (December):14–22.
Borba, Philip S., and Appel, David
  1987   "The Propensity of Permanently Disabled Workers to Hire Lawyers." *Industrial and Labor Relations Review* 40 (April):418–30.
Brealey, Richard, and Myers, Stewart
  1981   *Principles of Corporate Finance.* New York: McGraw-Hill.
Brechling, Frank
  1981   "Layoffs and Unemployment Insurance." In *Studies in Labor Markets*, edited by Sherwin Rosen, 187–207. Chicago: University of Chicago Press.
Brown, Charles
  1980   "Equalizing Differences in the Labor Market." *Quarterly Journal of Economics* (February):113–34.
Burkhauser, Richard V., and Haveman, Robert A.
  1982   *Disability and Work: The Economics of American Policy.* Baltimore: Johns Hopkins University Press.
Burton, John F., Jr.
  1983   "Compensation for Permanent Partial Disabilities." In *Safety and the Work Force*, edited by John D. Worrall, 18–60. Ithaca, N.Y.: ILR Press.
  1986   Appendix A: The Role of the Permanent Disability Rating Schedule in the Ontario Workers' Compensation Program. In Paul C. Weiler, "Permanent Partial Disability: Alternative Models for Compensation." Report prepared for the Ontario Minister of Labour, Ontario Ministry of Labour.

Burton, John F., Jr., and Berkowitz, Monroe
  1982   "The Role of the Workers' Compensation Program in Pro-
            moting Occupational Safety and Health." Report prepared for
            the Occupational Safety and Health Administration, U.S. De-
            partment of Labor.
Burton, John F., Jr., Hunt, H. Allan, and Krueger, Alan B.
  1985   *Interstate Variations in the Employers' Costs of Workers' Compen-*
            sation, with Particular Reference to Michigan and the Other
            Great Lake States. Ithaca, N.Y.: Workers' Disability Income
            Systems.
Burton, John F., Jr., and Krueger, Alan B.
  1986   "Interstate Variations in the Employers' Costs of Workers'
            Compensation, with Particular Reference to Connecticut, New
            Jersey, and New York." In *Current Issues in Workers' Compen-*
            sation, edited by James Chelius. Kalamazoo, Mich.: W. E. Up-
            john Institute for Employment Research.
Burton, John F., Jr., Partridge, Dane M., and Thomason, Terry
  1986   "Final Report of a Research Project on Nonscheduled Per-
            manent Partial Disability Benefits Provided by the New York
            State Workers' Compensation Program." Ithaca, N.Y.: New
            York State School of Industrial and Labor Relations, Cornell
            University. (Mimeo.)
Butler, Richard
  1983   "Wage and Injury Rate Response to Shifting Levels of
            Workers' Compensation." In *Safety and the Work Force*,
            edited by John D. Worrall, 61–86. Ithaca, N.Y.: ILR
            Press.
Butler, Richard, Kearl, J. R., and Worrall, John D.
  1984   "Rent Seeking in Workers' Compensation." (Mimeo.)
Butler, Richard, and Worrall, John D.
  1983   "Workers' Compensation: Benefit and Injury Claims Rates in
            the Seventies." *Review of Economics and Statistics* 60 (Novem-
            ber):580–89.
  1985   "Work Injury Compensation and the Duration of Nonwork
            Spells." *Economic Journal* 95 (September):714–24.
Chelius, James R.
  1973   "An Empirical Analysis of Safety Regulation." In *Supplemental*
            Studies for the National Commission on State Workmen's Compen-
            sation Laws, 3:53–66. Washington, D.C.: National Commission
            on State Workmen's Compensation.
  1974   "The Control of Industrial Accidents: Economic Theory and
            Empirical Evidence." *Law and Contemporary Problems* (Summer/
            Autumn):700–29.
  1976   "Liability for Industrial Accidents: A Comparison of Negli-
            gence and Strict Liability Systems." *Journal of Legal Studies* 5
            (June):293–309.

1977 *Workplace Safety and Health: The Role of Workers' Compensation,* Washington, D.C.: American Enterprise Institute.

1982 "The Influence of Workers' Compensation on Safety Incentives." *Industrial and Labor Relations Review* 35 (January):235–42.

Chelius, James R., and Smith, Robert S.

1983 "Experience-Rating and Injury Prevention." In *Safety and the Work Force,* edited by John D. Worrall, 128–37. Ithaca, N.Y.: ILR Press.

Crum and Forester's Occupational Disease Task Force

1983 "Role of the State Workers' Compensation System in Compensating Occupational Disease Victims." Morristown, N.J.: Crum and Forester. (Mimeo.)

Danziger, Sheldon, Haveman, Robert H., and Plotnick, Robert

1981 "How Income Transfer Programs Affect Work, Savings, and the Income Distribution: A Critical Review." *Journal of Economic Literature* 19:975–1028.

Dewees, Donald N.

1986 "Economic Incentives for Controlling Industrial Disease: The Asbestos Case." *Journal of Legal Studies* 15 (June):289–319.

Dewees, Donald N., and Daniels, Ronald J.

1986 "The Cost of Protecting Occupational Health: The Asbestos Case." *Journal of Human Resources* 21:381–96.

Dickens, William

1984 "Difference between Risk Premiums in Union and Nonunion Wages and the Case for Occupational Safety Regulation." *American Economic Review Papers and Proceedings* 96:320–23.

Dillingham, Alan E.

1983 "Demographic and Economic Change and the Costs of Workers' Compensation." In *Safety and the Work Force,* edited by John D. Worrall, 161–80. Ithaca, N.Y.: ILR Press.

Doherty, N.

1979 "National Insurance and Absence from Work." *Economic Journal* 89 (March):50–63.

Dorsey, Stuart

1983 "Employment Hazards and Fringe Benefits: Further Tests for Compensating Differentials." In *Safety and the Work Force,* edited by John D. Worrall, 87–102. Ithaca, N.Y.: ILR Press.

Dorsey, Stuart, and Walzer, Norman

1983 "Workers' Compensation, Job Hazards and Wages." *Industrial and Labor Relations Review* 36 (July):642–54.

Duncan, Greg, and Holmlund, Bertil

1983 "Was Adam Smith Right After All? Another Test of the Theory of Compensating Wage Differentials." *Journal of Labor Economics* 1 (October):366–79.

Duncan, Greg, and Stafford, Frank
 1980   "Do Union Members Receive Compensating Wage Differentials?" *American Economic Review* 70 (June):355–71.
Economic Report of the President
 1987   Washington, D.C.: Government Printing Office.
Ehrenberg, Ronald G., Hutchens, Robert, and Smith, Robert
 1978   "The Distribution of Unemployment Insurance Benefits and Costs." Technical Analysis Paper no. 58. Washington, D.C.: ASPER, U.S. Department of Labor.
Ehrenberg, Ronald G., and Oaxaca, Ronald
 1976   "Unemployment Insurance, Duration of Unemployment and Subsequent Wage Gain." *American Economic Review* 66 (December):754–67.
Ehrenberg, Ronald G., and Schumann, Paul
 1982   *Longer Hours or More Jobs? An Investigation of Amending Hours Legislation to Create Employment.* Ithaca, N.Y.: ILR Press.
 1984   "Compensating Wage Differentials for Mandatory Overtime." *Economic Inquiry* 22 (October):460–78.
Ehrenberg, Ronald G., and Smith, Robert
 1988   *Modern Labor Economics: Theory and Public Policy.* 3d ed. Glenwood, Ill.: Scott Foresman.
Farberow, N. L., et al.
 1966   "Suicide among Patients with Cardiorespiratory Illness." *Journal of the American Medical Association* 195 (February 7):128–34.
Fenn, Paul
 1981   "Sickness Duration, Residual Disability and Income Replacement: An Empirical Analysis." *Economic Journal* 91 (March):158–73.
Flinn, Chris, and Heckman, James
 1982   "Models for the Analysis of Labor Force Dynamics." In *Advances in Econometrics* 1:35–95. New York: Cambridge University Press.
Freeman, Richard, and Medoff, James L.
 1981   "The Impact of Percent Organized on the Nonunion Wage." *Review of Economics and Statistics* 63 (November):561–72.
 1984   *What Do Unions Do?* New York: Basic Books.
Haveman, Robert, and Wolfe, Barbara
 1984a   "The Decline in Male Labor Force Participation: Comment." *Journal of Political Economy* 92 (June):532–41.
 1984b   "Disability Transfers and Early Retirement: A Causal Relationship." *Journal of Public Economics* 24 (June):47–66.
Haynes, R. Brian, et al.
 1976   "Improvement of Medication Compliance in Uncontrolled Hypertension." *Lancet* (June 12):1265–68.

Horowitz, Stanley
  1977   "A Model of Unemployment Insurance and the Work Test."
          Industrial and Labor Relations Review 30 (July):462–66.
Ibbotson, Roger G., and Sinquefield, Rex A.
  1979   Stocks, Bonds, Bills and Inflation: Historical Returns. Charlottes-
          ville, Va.: Financial Analysts Research Foundation.
Insurance Information Institute
  1983   Insurance Facts, 1983–1984 Edition: Property, Liability, Marine,
          Surety. New York: Insurance Information Institute.
Johnson, William
  1979   "Disability, Income Support and Social Insurance." In Disa-
          bility Policies and Government Programs, edited by Edward D.
          Berkowitz, 87–130. New York: Praeger.
  1983   "Work Disincentives of Benefit Payments." In Safety and the Work
          Force, edited by John D. Worrall, 138–53. Ithaca, N.Y.: ILR Press.
Kasper, Daniel M.
  1975   "An Alternative to Workmen's Compensation." Industrial and
          Labor Relations Review 28 (July):535–48.
Lampman, Robert J.
  1984   Social Welfare Spending: Accounting for Changes from 1950 to
          1978. Orlando, Fla.: Academic Press.
Lancaster, T.
  1979   "Econometric Methods for the Duration of Unemployment."
          Econometrica 47 (November):939–56.
Larson, Arthur
  1953   The Laws of Workmen's Compensation (with 1988 supplement).
          New York: Matthew Bender.
  1986   Unjust Dismissal (with 1988 supplement). New York: Matthew
          Bender.
Leonard, Jonathan
  1979   The Social Security Disability Program and Labor Force Participa-
          tion. Working Paper no. 392. Washington, D.C.: National Bu-
          reau of Economic Research.
MacAvoy, Paul
  1982   "The Economic Consequences of Asbestos Related Diseases."
          Working Paper no. 27. New Haven, Conn.: Yale School of
          Organization and Management.
Mashaw, Jerry
  1983   Bureaucratic Justice: Managing Social Security Disability Claims.
          New Haven, Conn.: Yale University Press.
Mashaw, Jerry L., et al.
  1978   Social Security Hearings and Appeals. Lexington, Mass.: Lexing-
          ton Books.
McMillan, Alma W., and Bixby, Ann K.
  1980   "Social Welfare Expenditures, Fiscal Year 1978." Social Security
          Bulletin 43 (May):3–17.

Ministry for Social Affairs and Employment
    1982   *Social Security in the Netherlands.* The Hague: Ministry for Social
           Affairs and Employment.
Mitchell, Daniel J. B.
    1985   "The Changing American Workplace." *Labor Lawyer* 1
           (Spring):301–20.
Moore, Michael J., and Viscusi, W. Kip
    1987   "The Impact of Errors of Measurement and Ability Bias
           on Estimates of Compensating Wage Differentials: Evi-
           dence from Panel Data." Working Paper 87–5. Durham,
           N.C.: Duke University, Center for the Study of Business
           Regulation.
Munnell, Alicia H.
    1982   *The Economics of Private Pensions.* Washington, D.C.: Brookings
           Institution.
National Commission on State Workmen's Compensation Laws
    1972   *Report of the National Commission on State Workmen's Compensation*
           Laws. Washington, D.C.: Government Printing Office.
    1973   *Supplemental Studies for the National Commission on State Work-*
           men's Compensation Laws. Washington: D.C.: Government
           Printing Office.
National Legal Center for the Public Interest
    1981   *Proceedings of the National Conference on Workers' Compensation*
           and Workplace Liability. Washington, D.C.: National Legal Cen-
           ter for the Public Interest.
New York Temporary State Commission on Workers' Compensation and
Disability Benefits
    1986   *Final Report of the Temporary State Commission on Workers' Com-*
           pensation and Disability Benefits. Albany, N.Y.
Olson, Craig
    1981   "An Analysis of Wage Differentials Received by Workers on
           Dangerous Jobs." *Journal of Human Resources* 16 (Spring):167–
           85.
Parsons, Donald
    1980a   "The Decline in Male Labor Force Participation." *Journal of*
           Political Economy 88 (February):117–34.
    1980b   "Racial Trends in Male Labor Force Participation." *American*
           Economic Review 70 (December):911–20.
    1984   "Disability Insurance and Male Labor Force Participation: A
           Response to Haveman and Wolfe." *Journal of Political Economy*
           92 (June):542–49.
Peto, Julian, Henderson, Brian E., and Pike, Malcolm C.
    1981   "Trends in Mesothelioma Incidence in the United States and
           the Forecast Epidemic Due to Asbestos Exposure during
           World War II." In *Quantification of Occupational Cancer,* Ban-
           bury Report 9, edited by Richard Peto and Marvin Schnei-

derman, 51–72. Cold Spring Harbor, N.Y.: Cold Spring Harbor Laboratory.

Price, Daniel
- 1979   "Workers' Compensation Programs in 1970s." *Social Security Bulletin* 42 (May):3–24.
- 1984a   "Cash Benefits for Short-Term Sickness, 1948–81." *Social Security Bulletin* 47 (August):23–38.
- 1984b   "Workers' Compensation: Coverage, Benefits and Costs, 1982." *Social Security Bulletin* 47 (December):7–13.
- 1986   "Workers' Compensation: Coverage, Benefits, and Costs, 1984." *Social Security Bulletin* 49 (December):19–24.

Robinson, Cynthia, Lemen, Richard A., and Wagoner, Joseph K.
- 1979   "Mortality Patterns, 1940–1975, among Workers Employed in an Asbestos Textile, Friction and Packing Products Manufacturing Facility." In *Dusts and Disease*, edited by Richard A. Lemen and John M. Dement. Park Forest South, Ill.: Pathotox.

Royal Commission on Asbestos
- 1984   *Report of the Royal Commission on Matters of Health and Safety Arising from the Use of Asbestos in Ontario.* Toronto: Queens Printer.

Ruser, John W.
- 1985   "Workers' Compensation Insurance, Experience Rating and Occupational Injuries." *Rand Journal of Economics* 16 (Winter):487–503.
- 1986   "Measuring Wage Premiums for Job Risks." *Monthly Labor Review* (June):42–43.

Sackett, David L., et al.
- 1975   "Randomized Clinical Trial of Strategies for Improving Medication Compliance in Primary Hypertension." *Lancet* (May 31):1205–7.

Sakinofsky, I.
- 1980   "Depression and Suicide in the Disabled." In *Behavioral Problems in the Disabled*, edited by D. S. Bishop, 16–51. Baltimore: Williams and Wilkins.

Selikoff, Irving
- 1981   *Disability Compensation for Asbestos-Associated Disease in the U.S.* New York: Environmental Sciences Laboratory, Mt. Sinai School of Medicine.

Simon, William H.
- 1983   "Legality, Bureaucracy, and Class in the Welfare System." *Yale Law Journal* 92 (June):1198–269.

Smith, Kent
- 1977   "Psychological Implications of Pulmonary Disease." *Clinical Notes on Respiratory Disease* 16:3–11.

Smith, Robert
- 1979   "Compensating Wage Differentials and Public Policy: A Review." *Industrial and Labor Relations Review* (April):339–52.

Smith, Robert, and Dillingham, Alan
    1984   "Union Effects on the Valuation of Fatal Risk." *Proceedings of the Thirty-Sixth Annual Meeting of the Industrial Relations Research Association.* Madison, Wisc.: Industrial Relations Research Association.

Solon, Gary
    1984   "The Effects of Unemployment Insurance Eligibility Rules on Job Quitting Behavior." *Journal of Human Resources* 19 (Winter):118–27.

Somers, Herman M., and Somers, Anne R.
    1954   *Workmen's Compensation: Prevention Insurance and Rehabilitation of Occupational Disability.* New York: John Wiley and Sons.

Sunshine, J.
    1980   "Disability: A Comprehensive Overview of Programs, Issues, and Options for Change." Report prepared for President's Commission on Pension Policy.

Thompson, J. A.
    1979   "Implementing Workmen's Compensation Programs in the States: The Influence of Organizational Characteristics and Exogenous Factors on Policy Effectiveness." (Mimeo.)
    1980   "The Determinants of State Workmen's Compensation Laws." In *Employment and Labor Relations Policy,* edited by Charles Bulmer and John L. Carmichael, Jr., 193–210. Lexington, Mass.: Lexington Books.

Topel, Robert
    1983   "On Layoffs and Unemployment Insurance." *American Economic Review* 83 (September):541–60.

U.S. Bureau of the Census
    1984   *Statistical Abstract of the United States: 1985.* Washington, D.C.: Government Printing Office.

U.S. Chamber of Commerce
    1983   *Employee Benefits, 1982.* Washington, D.C.

U.S. Department of Education
    1981   *Basic Grants: End of Year Report, 1979–80.* Washington, D.C.: Government Printing Office.

U.S. Department of Labor
    1979a   *Workers' Compensation Reform: Challenge for the 80's.* Research Report of the Interdepartmental Workers' Compensation Task Force, vol. 1.
    1979b   *Promptness of Payment in Workers' Compensation.* Research Report of the Interdepartmental Workers' Compensation Task Force, vol. 3.
    1985   *State Compliance with the Nineteen Essential Recommendations of the National Commission on State Workmen's Compensation Laws, 1972–1984.* Washington, D.C.: Employment Standards Administration, Division of State Workers' Compensation Programs.

1988   *State Compliance with the Nineteen Essential Recommendations of the National Commission on State Workmen's Compensation Laws, 1972–84.* Washington, D.C.: Employment Standards Administration, Division of State Workers' Compensation Programs.

1988b   *State Workers' Compensation Laws in Effect on January 1, 1988 Compared with the Nineteen Essential Recommendations of the National Commission on State Workmen's Compensation Laws.* Washington, D.C.: Employment Standards Administration, Division of State Workers' Compensation Programs.

Victor, Richard
1983   *Workers' Compensation and Workplace Safety: The Nature of Employer Financial Incentives.* Santa Monica, Calif.: Rand Corp.

Victor, Richard, Cohen, Linda, and Phelps, Charles
1982   *Workers' Compensation and Workplace Safety: Employer Response to Financial Incentives.* Santa Monica, Calif.: Rand Corp.

Viscusi, W. Kip
1978   "Wealth and Effects and Earnings Premium for Job Hazards." *Review of Economics and Statistics* 60 (August):408–16.

1979   *Employment Hazards: An Investigation of Market Performance.* Cambridge, Mass.: Harvard University Press.

1980   "Union Labor Market Structure and the Welfare Implications of the Quality of Work." *Journal of Labor Research* 1 (Spring):175–92.

Viscusi, W. Kip, and Moore, Michael J.
1987   "Workers' Compensation: Wage Effects, Benefit Inadequacies, and the Value of Health Loss." *Review of Economics and Statistics* 69 (May):249–61.

Vroman, Wayne
1982   "Permanent Disabling Injuries: A General Model and an Application to Florida Work Injuries." *Advances in Health Economics and Health Services Research* 3 (1982):235–81.

Weiler, Paul M.
1980   "Reshaping Workers' Compensation for Ontario." Report submitted to Robert G. Elgie, M.D., Minister of Labour, Ontario Ministry of Labour.

1983   "Protecting the Worker from Disability: Challenges for the Eighties." Report submitted to Russell H. Ramsay, Minister of Labour, Ontario Ministry of Labour.

Williams, C. Arthur, Turnbull, John G., and Chelt, Earl F.
1982   *Economics and Social Security: Social Insurance and Other Approaches.* 5th ed. New York: John Wiley and Sons.

"Workmen's Compensation Payments and Costs, 1957"
1958   *Social Security Bulletin* 21 (December):17–18.

"Workmen's Compensation Payments and Costs, 1961"
1963   *Social Security Bulletin* 33 (January):27, 28, 37–41.

"Workmen's Compensation Payments and Costs, 1968"
  1970   *Social Security Bulletin* 33 (January):33–36.
Worrall, John D.
  1983   "Compensation Costs, Injury Rates, and the Labor Market."
          In *Safety and the Work Force: Incentives and Disincentives in Work-
          ers' Compensation,* edited by John D. Worrall, 1–17. Ithaca,
          N.Y.: ILR Press.
Worrall, John, D., and Appel, David
  1982   "The Wage Replacement Rate and Benefit Utilization in
          Workers' Compensation." *Journal of Risk and Insurance* 49 (Sep-
          tember):361–71.
  1985   "Some Benefit Issues in Workers' Compensation." In *Workers'
          Compensation Benefits: Adequacy, Equity, and Efficiency,* edited by
          John D. Worrall and David Appel, 1–18. Ithaca, N.Y.: ILR
          Press.
Worrall, John, and Butler, Richard
  1983   "Health Conditions and Job Hazards: Union and Nonunion
          Jobs." *Journal of Labor Research* (Fall):340–46.
  1985   "Workers' Compensation: Benefits and Duration of Claims."
          In *Workers' Compensation Benefits: Adequacy, Equity, and Effi-
          ciency,* edited by John D. Worrall and David Appel, 57–70.
          Ithaca, N.Y.: ILR Press.
Worrall, John, Butler, Richard, Borba, Philip, and Durbin, David
  1985   "Age and Incentive Response: Illinois Low Back Workers'
          Compensation Claims." (Mimeo.)

INDEX

CONTRIBUTORS

John F. Burton, Jr., is a professor in the New York State School of Industrial and Labor Relations, Cornell University. He received his LL.B. and Ph.D. from the University of Michigan. He has published extensively on the workers' compensation program and served as the chairman of the National Commission on State Workmen's Compensation Laws from 1971 to 1972.

Donald N. Dewees is a professor of economics and law at the University of Toronto. He received his LL.B. and Ph.D. from Harvard University. He served as the director of research for the Ontario Royal Commission on Asbestos from 1980 to 1984.

Ronald G. Ehrenberg is the Irving M. Ives Professor of Industrial and Labor Relations in the New York State School of Industrial and Labor Relations, Cornell University. He received his Ph.D. from Northwestern University. A research associate at the National Bureau of Economic Research, he is the author of more than seventy-five articles and books.

Robert M. Hutchens is chairman of the Department of Labor Economics in the New York State School of Industrial and Labor Relations, Cornell University. He received his Ph.D. from the University of Wisconsin. He has written extensively on labor economics, social insurance and public assistance, and public finance.

Robert J. Lampman is professor emeritus of economics at the University of Wisconsin, where he received his Ph.D. His writings include *Social Welfare Spending: Accounting for Changes from 1950 to 1978*. He has served as a member of the executive committee of the American Economic Association.

Arthur Larson is the James B. Duke Professor at the Duke University Law School. A Rhodes scholar, he received a doctor of civil laws from Oxford University. His writings include *The Law of Workmen's Compensation* and, with Lex Larson, *The Law of Employment Discrimination*. He has served as the undersecretary of labor, director of the U.S. Information Agency, and special assistant to President Dwight Eisenhower.

John Lewis is an attorney in Coconut Grove, Florida. A graduate of the Duke University Law School, he has served as a consultant to private and public organizations involved in workers' compensation reform and as the associate executive director and chief counsel of the National Commission on State Workmen's Compensation Laws.

Jerry L. Mashaw is the William Nelson Cromwell Professor of Law at Yale University and a professor in the Yale Institute for Social and Policy Studies. He received his J.D. degree from Tulane University and his Ph.D. from the University of Edinburgh. He is the author of several books, including *Bureaucratic Justice* and *Due Process in the Administrative State*.